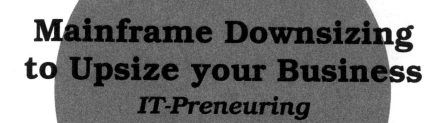

Mainframe Downsizing to Upsize your Business
IT-Preneuring

James B. M. Grosvenor

Contributing Authors:
Utsumi Ichiro and Patricia A. O'Brien

PTR Prentice Hall
Englewood Cliffs, New Jersey 07632

Library of Congress Cataloging-in-Publication Data
Grosvenor, James B. M.
    Mainframe downsizing to upsize your business: IT-preneuring /
James B. M. Grosvenor.
        p.   cm.
    Includes index.
    ISBN 0-13-102708-5
    1. Management information systems. 2. Electronic data processing -
    -Distributed systems   I. Title.
HD30.213.G76   1994
658.4'038'011--dc20   93-37374
                                             CIP

Editorial/production supervison
        and interior design: *Camille Trentacoste*
Production coordinator: *Alexis Heydt*
Acquisitions editor: *Paul Becker*
Editorial assistant: *Maureen Diana*
Cover design: *Design Solutions*

 © 1994 by PTR Prentice Hall
Prentice-Hall, Inc.
A Paramount Communications Company
Englewood Cliffs, New Jersey 07632

The publisher offers discounts on this book when ordered in bulk quantities.
For more information, contact:

        Corporate Sales Department
        PTR Prentice Hall
        113 Sylvan Avenue
        Englewood Cliffs, NJ 07632

        Phone: 201-592-2863
        FAX: 201-592-2249

Printed in the United States of America
10 9 8 7 6 5 4 3 2 1

ISBN 0-13-102708-5

Prentice-Hall International (UK) Limited, *London*
Prentice-Hall of Australia Pty. Limited, *Sydney*
Prentice-Hall Canada Inc., *Toronto*
Prentice-Hall Hispanoamericana, S.A., *Mexico*
Prentice-Hall of India Private Limited, *New Delhi*
Prentice-Hall of Japan, Inc., *Tokyo*
Simon & Schuster Asia Pte. Ltd., *Singapore*
Editora Prentice-Hall do Brasil, Ltda., *Rio de Janeiro*

To my son, JimmyYuji

Contents

Preface

This book heralds the opening of a new era of computing...an era during which information systems break out of the central glass house and are transformed into powerful, intelligent networks harnessed by people in organizations around the globe to do their jobs more effectively. Many of the MIS directors interviewed over the last two months for this book, radiated with excitement as they described the dawning of a new era in their own MIS departments. Budgets are being cut in half by discarding old paradigm mainframes ("Delight Inc.," "Mediply"), MIS staff are changing from tech gurus into high-tech business consultants ("Liteline," Simmonds Precision), and users are taking the lead in designing information infrastructures to beat the competition (Yokogawa Electric, American Airlines).

Bob Beegen, MIS Director at Paychex, could have been mistaken for a Silicon Valley entrepreneur as he mapped out a plan for injecting the newer distributed computing technologies to spawn new Paychex businesses targeting small business owners. The emergence of managers who have honed both their business and information systems skills, and are leveraging cross-disciplinary experience to build competitive advantages for their company, provides us with the opportunity to coin a phrase to describe this new breed of manager. How about IT-preneur? Entrepreneurs create new businesses out of ideas. Intrapreneurs cut across bureaucratic red tape to create or expand businesses within suffocating bureaucracies. IT-preneurs work in both small businesses and large corporate worlds to unleash the power of information technology on business problems, and to use that power to often create completely new businesses.

IT-preneurs come from various walks of life and different parts of the globe. The business manager now is becoming part programmer as he learns to use "object agents" to fetch his daily stock market, sales order, and cost variance reports. MIS staff members are becoming strategists as they jointly build business plans with their business counterparts to justify the installation of newer systems. Many of these plans include projected revenues to be derived from enhanced business activities supported by the new systems (not typical MIS techno-speak). This phenomenon is not limited to the U.S., it stretches as far away as Japan, a country even more shackled by proprietary mainframe systems. Japanese managers are looking to U.S. vendors and software houses to release them from mainframe bondage, and help them enter a new computing world of greater price performance and flexibility.

This book is written for all of the above managers, the business manager turning IT strategist, the MIS manager turning business strategist, the U.S. manager looking to global markets, and the Japanese manager looking to the U.S. for guidance (it is being published in both Japanese and English languages). Moreover, this book provides insights into the Japanese market for U.S. producers of software downsizing enablers, such as CASE tools, client/server applications, and multivendor networking utilities, that will prove useful as they set their sights on penetrating the vast and growing Japanese market. The same is true for Japanese software houses looking to connect up with their U.S. counterparts to bring these new technologies to Japan.

The value of the information in this volume is both fleeting and enduring. This book will undoubtedly endure over time as a snapshot taken at a point of dynamic transition in both the computing and business worlds. Some managers view the usurping of mainframe empires by midrange and PC LANs as commensurate with the falling of the Berlin Wall and the collapse of the Soviet Union (which was also based on mainframe-like central control). IT and business management historians can look to this book in years to come for answering their questions on how it all began...to relive the frustrations and exhilaration of managers implementing a technology change packed with enough capability to shatter the very power balance of major corporations. In the recent past, many well-known U.S. companies were driven "by the numbers" to such an extent that it was often difficult to tell the difference between CFOs and CEOs. The newly emerging MIS role as a generator of true competitive advantage, may soon lead to a similar blurring of CEO and CIO roles.

Information in this book of a more fleeting nature includes the descriptions of recent software and hardware releases, the comparisons of different vendor products, the "how to" prescriptions for such tasks as migrating programs and EBCIDIC code off the mainframe, and vendor names and rankings. Vendor rankings, for instance, are subject to frequent change due to such events as the sudden appearance of rapid growth start-ups, and the failure or merger of major players, all commonplace in this industry. These fleeting-value items are all of burning interest to MIS managers trying to move with the times today...but are likely to seem like yesterday's news to them in a few years. All are candidates for updating in future editions.

Those of you who glanced at the inside cover and noticed that I work for HP may wonder whether you will be subjected to HP marketing pitches throughout this work. Just as a warning, the HP pitch is included in Chapter 6, under the section heading, "Which Hardware Vendor to Choose," I have tried my best to contain my unbridled enthusiasm for HP products throughout the rest of the book. Before turning to Chapter 6, however, I would suggest first reading the accounts of HP customers in the other chapters. All customers have had an opportunity to review and adjust the stories appearing in this book to reflect their true views.

Others who read my biography further may have noticed that my background is anything but highly technical. I graduated from Harvard in East Asian Languages and Civilizations, earned an MBA at Wharton in finance, and managed top management consulting projects in numerous industries (including the computer industry) for McKinsey and Company in Tokyo and Los Angeles for five years. Subsequently, I joined HP, and over the past five years have worked in various capacities as an internal consultant to top management members. HP projects have ranged from structuring partnerships with U.S. software houses, to developing and implementing HP's commercial systems strategy in Japan. I am now launching a U.S.-based project to ensure HP is the "best company for commercial systems customers to work with." The writing of this book was taken on to share with potential HP customers some of the insights I and other HP managers have gained from participating in the rapidly changing U.S. and Japanese markets.

Why read a "technical book" written by a non-technical manager? The fact is that many of the most intractable issues of information technology are non-technical. Having the perfect technical solution for a company's information infrastructure does not guarantee a successful implementation. Communicating a solution to sponsoring business managers in terms they understand, avoiding excessive friction with managers and employees suffering from IT culture shock as new technologies alter their job descriptions, convincing long-term mainframe MIS employees that the UNIX® "hackers" they have viewed as the nemesis of the computing world can actually teach them something (and vice versa), are not dealt with in sufficient depth in most computer books. I have tried to leverage my non-technical background to fill in these gaps, and worked with my technical colleagues inside and outside HP to bridge back to the computer world.

The truth is, however, that I am no stranger to computers. I caught the computer "bug" very early in life, but it has been dormant throughout much of my career. A very generous alumnus of the high school I attended (St. George's School in Newport, Rhode Island) donated a DEC PDP 8/s for students to engage in intellectual pursuit. Very little formal instruction was provided, and so those of us who were interested had the computer to ourselves. A friend of mine, Henry Dupont, and I spent day and night tickling the computer's innards and writing programs in Fortran and machine language. We even developed a reverse assembler for satiating our curiosity about the source code of the Fortran compiler, and used it to print out the whole compiler for hours of subroutine-chasing entertainment. Henry sold the reverse assembler to DEC before graduating from St. George's.

I did not put computers aside due to lack of interest. On the contrary, I was so overwhelmed by the way computers consumed all of my waking hours that I decided I had to kick the habit or never get anything else done. Luckily, thanks to HP, I have been able to return to the computer industry, and now share part of that experience with the readers of this book.

By the way, if any of you have insights into how HP can truly become the "best company" for you to work with, I would greatly appreciate hearing from you.

> Jim Grosvenor
> Hewlett-Packard 46UU
> 19091 Pruneridge Ave.
> Cupertino, CA 95014

Acknowledgments

The people to whom I owe the most gratitude are the numerous MIS managers, directors, and other individuals, who shared their experiences with me, reviewed and corrected my numerous drafts, and then became champions within their own companies to obtain approval for publishing their stories. Thanks to the efforts of these individuals, most of the company examples appear with actual company names included. Even the interviewees at companies choosing to appear in disguised form, spent much time ensuring their stories were accurately presented. These managers did not want unwary readers to be misled as they chart their own migrations off of mainframes. Unfortunately, the names of these selfless contributors could not be included in the text.

I also want to extend my heartfelt thanks to the contributing authors listed on the cover of this book, Patricia O'Brien and Utsumi Ichiro. Ms. O'Brien, at the time a manager in HP's Mainframe Alternative Program and now assigned to the Client/Server program, helped conduct some of the interviews and drafted several portions of the book, including most of Chapter 5, "The Tricky Question of Moving the Software," and portions of Chapter 7, including the section entitled, "Where Are The Tools To Create This Client/Server World?"

My gratitude to Utsumi Ichiro, a well-known and prolific author in Japan, is of a different nature. I can truly say that without Utsumi-san I would not have written this book. Although he has not written a word of the English text, he inspired me to take on the seemingly impossible challenge of authoring my first book in a couple of short months. My affiliation with Utsumi-san was spawned by stumbling across some of his thought-provoking and informative books (written in Japanese) concerning the dynamics of the Japanese computer industry. I was impressed by his characterization of Japanese vendor, software house, and end user issues in his books, and called him from the U.S. to ask if I could retain him as a consultant. I needed well-informed advice as I worked with the management teams of Hewlett-Packard and Yokogawa Hewlett-Packard to refine HP's Japanese computer systems strategy.

As an independent writer of many books on the computer industry, and an editor/publisher of a Japanese periodical entitled "Software Business," Utsumi-san would not accept any payment for his advice, for fear of becoming too closely affiliated with a particular hardware vendor. Nevertheless, we met many times in Japan, spent countless evenings roaming the streets and drinking establishments of Ginza and Akasaka, and interviewed, through Utsumi-san's generous introduction, many of the leading thinkers in the Japanese software and hardware industries. It was on one of those late-night drinking sprees that Utsumi-san suggested we co-author a book. I agreed that evening, and discovered the next day that he had already found a publisher. To my surprise, he had agreed with the publisher to submit a draft in a few months' time.

I owe much to Utsumi-san. Not only was he the catalyst that drove me to create the book you now hold in your hands, he was a creative brainstorming partner, with whom I developed many of the perspectives on the Japanese computer industry described in Chapter 1. Those of you who are reading the Japanese version of this book, will see his handicraft in the polished Japanese to which he converted my crude Japanese translation of roughly half the text. I ran out of time and could not finish the entire translation. The remainder was translated by professional translators and was also refined by Utsumi-san's gifted hand.

Finally, I owe a great deal to Hewlett-Packard, and to Rick Justice, the General Manager in charge of HP's Asia Pacific Computer Systems Organization. He allowed me to pull away from my Japanese Strategy implementation program, and funded my efforts for writing the book. During a time of squeezed profits and tight deadlines, few top management members find it easy to support efforts that may not link to "hard" revenues over the next few quarters. Rick Justice had the foresight and generosity to invest in this effort, an effort which should hopefully benefit users of information systems, regardless of whether they choose to become HP customers or not.

There are, of course, many others who contributed in numerous ways to the creation of this book. I hope they will forgive me if I do not call them out by name here, but instead, thank them ensemble profusely for their efforts.

The Downsizing Revolution

Saving Your Job by Making "Crazy" Downsizing Decisions

Burlington Coat Factory

"System Down!" yelled one of Mike Prince's ten PL1 programmers at Burlington Coat Factory's New Hampshire Information Systems center. The 3-4 MIPs Honeywell mainframe had inexplicably crashed, bringing all information systems operations to a screeching halt. The system engineers rushed to make adjustments to Burlington's home-grown database software (operating on the Dartmouth College-originated DTTS operating system), and reboot the system. The rest decided to take an early lunch because no work could be done in the interim.

The year was 1984. Mr. Prince pulled out the new store expansion plan and wondered how his IS department was going to keep up with the tremendous growth projected for the Burlington Coat chain (20 to 50, and then to several hundred stores in just a few years). Order-processing volumes during peak winter months already took up much of the system capacity, and Mr. Prince did not like the prospect of upgrading the mainframe.

The expansion plan was even more problematic for Burlington Coat than for most retailers because it had chosen not to set up a central distribution center. Instead, Burlington asked suppliers to drop off merchandise directly at the stores. On the surface, this system appeared to reduce work by cutting out a step in the distribution process. Mr. Prince, however, saw paperwork and transactions proliferating across the mainframe network with every additional store opening. He could easily see that the entire system would be crippled if the chain were to grow beyond 50 stores.

Burlington Coat was not the type of company to throw money at a problem hoping it would go away. Burlington makes money as a chain that sells brand merchandise for less. To deliver low prices to the customer, Burlington has to maintain one of the lowest cost distribution and retail organizations in the industry.

Mr. Prince's staff had invested years developing virtually all of their applications on the mainframe in-house. As mentioned above, even their database software was homegrown. Their dependence on the mainframe was becoming bothersome as they saw innovations on other computer platforms introduced sooner, and at lower cost, than the proprietary platform they had "married" years before. Mr. Prince felt trapped.

His opportunity came in 1989 with the company decision to create a $20 million distribution hub. He was tasked with not only constructing an information system to manage the new distribution center processes, but also with ensuring easy expansion of system capacity to support the expected rise in business volume. Few in the company had any notion of what the volumes might be.

His next decision was considered "crazy" by many on Burlington's board of directors and almost cost him his job. He installed a scalable UNIX Sequent server system linked to UNIX workstations, X-terminals, and PCs (the network protocol was TCP/IP). In an effort to protect what he saw as a perfectly logical move given the environment and Burlington Coat's information needs, Mr. Prince brought in an influential consultant from Silicon Valley to advise top management on IS technology. He assumed that the consultant would help the management team see his recent decisions in a more positive light. To his dismay, the consultant joined the ranks of nay-sayers and claimed that moving away from the proprietary mainframe environment and betting Burlington's business on a relatively untested UNIX system was too risky.

Mr. Prince's hot seat got hotter with the company's sudden decision to add a linen line to their business. Burlington's system, which had processed, for the most part, outerwear transactions of over

$100-200 each, now all of a sudden was deluged with a plethora of $1-2 transactions. The transaction volume for the linen business alone soon equaled the volume of all other product lines together. The homegrown accounting system on the mainframe was clearly ripping apart at the seams.

It is unlikely that Mr. Prince would have been able to survive these transitions without the backing of two insightful and influential management members. Monroe Milstein, Chairman, and Mark Nesci, then VP of Operations (now Chief Operating Officer), worked closely with Mr. Prince as he mulled over whether to use more traditional technologies from DEC, or take the leap to Sequent. Mr. Prince's strong conviction that the UNIX path was best for Burlington's business, the compelling logic of the open systems arguments, and unfaltering support from these two management members, allowed Burlington Coat Factory to be one of the first companies to break ground with open systems.

Mr. Prince discovered a new freedom with the UNIX platform. He was not locked into developing a completely new accounting system for Burlington's evolving needs. He tested out some of the new UNIX applications from a fast-growing Silicon Valley relational database company, Oracle, and found Oracle held its own against mainframe applications. Mr. Prince's next "crazy" purchase decision led Burlington to be the first customer of Oracle's Accounts Payable package.

Mr. Prince doesn't hear much from nay-sayers anymore. The company has expanded without major glitches to 168 stores today and has plans to reach 185 stores in the fall. The scalable UNIX platform has allowed Burlington to easily expand capacity throughout the period of high growth, to shift processes from batch to more responsive OLTP (On-Line Transaction Processing), and convert from terrestrial to satellite wide area networking.

Mr. Prince's next surprise came with the introduction of a clearly superior mainframe retail package that was snapped up by Burlington's competitors. To his dismay, the package could only run in the mainframe environment. He felt that it was ironic that the open systems path he had chosen was now blocking him from a competitive product.

A quick investigation of his options revealed that the world had now turned full loop. Another start-up called Integris came to his rescue with a package that provides CICS Cobol mainframe environment capabilities on UNIX platforms. Mr. Prince says he now runs the mainframe package without speed degradation on the UNIX platform using Integris.

Today, as Mr. Prince watches many of his CIO counterparts being shown the door for not sufficiently aligning their information systems with company business needs, he realizes that many of the decisions he made, in fact, saved his career.

Who Else Is Downsizing?

Burlington Coat Factory was on the cutting edge of downsizing. Today, a few short years after Burlington Coat started their transformation, virtually every large U.S. company has begun, or is investigating the feasibility of an information system downsizing effort. Of 75 Fortune 1000 companies recently surveyed by Forrester Research, only 4% said they were not interested in downsizing. This observation is further substantiated by a 1992 survey conducted by WorkGroup Technologies, Inc. of 110 U.S. MIS managers, many of whom clearly have their sights on making significant changes in the structure of their IS budgets. According to the survey results, IS managers expect to reduce their mainframe-related expenditures from 40% of their total IS budgets in 1991 to 27% by 1995. Just to get a feel for the magnitude of this change, let's assume continued 6% annual growth in U.S. computer spending overall and apply the above projected budget shift to the entire market. Given these assumptions, the projected mainframe market declines by a whopping 20% (approximately $8 billion) over this time frame. It is unlikely that the entire market will move with such speed, but even if half the market changes over, it still translates into sizable declines in mainframes purchased. IBM, the dominant market shareowner of this rapidly declining U.S. market is already ailing seriously. IBM recently recorded a revenue decline (5%) for the first time since 1946 and a deficit ($2.8 billion), the first in IBM's history.

Research firms are projecting mainframe market downturns that are less severe. International Data Corp., for instance, expects the "Large Computer" share of the U.S. computer market to decline from 19% in 1990 to 17% in 1995, but to increase in absolute terms at a CAGR of 3.2% over the same period. Major discontinuities in the computer industry are nevertheless notoriously difficult to project accurately.

Types of Downsizing Companies

The list of "Downsizing Companies" in Table 1-1 was compiled from articles appearing in U.S. computer periodicals during 1991/92. This list includes, of course, only those companies willing to disclose the details of their downsizing programs to reporters. Often, companies refuse interviews to avoid leaking downsizing secrets to competitors. There appears to be little rhyme or reason to the list. The downsizing companies listed here compete in all industries, are of all sizes, and provide all types of products and services.

These companies are reducing their MIS budgets by phenomenal amounts. The downsizing path represented by this sample is varied, including companies going straight to PC LANs, and others moving to midrange proprietary and UNIX server platforms.

The results of a May, 1993, HP survey of 300 HP and non-HP customers gives us a better feel for the types of platforms to which U.S. companies are downsizing (Figure 1-1). Of the respondents who were aggressively moving work off mainframes, 65% were moving mainframe data and applications to PC networks. Other popular downsizing platforms are workstation/PC client/server networks (53%) and midrange/workstation configurations (43%).

But are these downsizers moving to open systems platforms? Apparently more than half (59%) are aggressive movers to open systems as well. This corroborates other evidence in this book (Chapter 6) that UNIX has come into its own as a platform for commercial applications. To what extent, however, are UNIX systems being entrusted with mission-critical applications? To get a feel for how many applications being installed on UNIX are of a time-critical operations nature, I grouped UNIX user responses to a survey question (included in the Workgroup Technologies survey mentioned above) asking respondents to list new applications being placed on downsized servers into three general categories: less time-critical decision support, more time-critical operations, and unclear (Table 1-2). The breakdown between less time-critical and more time-critical is about fifty-fifty, with slightly more UNIX applications falling in the time-critical operations category. Responses in the Unclear column such as "Everything" and "Strategic Applications" could be legitimately shifted over to the operations category as well, and tip the scale even more toward more time-critical applications.

Table 1-1: Downsizing Companies Appearing in 1991/1992 U.S. Press Articles

Company Name	Downsizing Story
JFK Medical Center	Substituted RISC network for mainframe, saved 25% of IS staff expense and several $100,000 in HW/SW cost.[a]
Foxboro	Downsized to HP systems and reduced annual IS budget from $27.7 million to $15 million. Reduced IS staff from 225 to 115.[b]
Paragon Steak House	Saved more than $1 million by moving to HP-UX. Can now run a $150 million operation with six people. Did not convert…rather used VIS/TP to emulate in UNIX environment.[c]
CBS/FOX Video	Reduced MIS budget from $2.8 million to $800,000 and reduced MIS staff of 23 to 5 through downsizing.[d]
American Sterilizer	Cut HW and SW costs by 75%. (MIS budget was $1.6 million in 1985, $.9 million in 1988, and $.3 million in 1990.) Accounts receivable were converted from mainframe to PC network in two months. IBM 4341/IBM4381 changed to model P3-centered structure.[e]
G. Heileman Brewing	Amdahl MF and IBM 3090 downsized to two Pyramid servers (saved several million dollars per year).[f]
Keyport Life Insurance	Moved from two IBM mainframes to Net Frame 450 SuperServer and saved $1.3 million (the budget now is $5 million).[g]
Butler-Cox Foundation	Downsizing from mainframe to client server will reduce ownership costs 20% to 30% over five years.[h]
J.M Huber Corp	Will phase out an IBM 3090 and run Oracle on RS6000s.[i]
Georgia-Pacific	Converted 6600 programs from mainframes to AS/400s. Sold the mainframes for scrap and received only $6,000 each.[j]
Merrill Lynch	Reduced mainframe compute cycle expense from $2 million/year to less than $1 million.[k]
Appraiser's Office (Orange County, Florida)	Mainframe moved to PC network and cut costs from $1.8 million to $800,000.[l]

6

Table 1-1: Downsizing Companies Appearing in 1991/1992 U.S. Press Articles (Continued)

Company Name	Downsizing Story
TRW	Unplugged an IBM4381 for annual savings of $10 million.[m]
Motorola	Selling all mainframes this year. Have been able to drop IS budget as a percent of revenue from 5% last year to 1.6% this year. Goal is to have it below 1% by end of 1993, and to have it all on UNIX.[n]
Texas Rehab Comm	Migrating claims processing from mainframes to UNIX servers and Netware LANs, for cost savings of $7.5 million over five years.[o]
Pepsico	Has not had a major system developed for a mainframe for at least a year. PC population has grown from 2,000 to 16,000 units installed.[p]
Duke Power	Spending as few dollars on the mainframe as possible, moving processing cycles to less expensive platforms.[q]

a. *Information Week*, Feb. 10 1992
b. *Schussel's Downsizing Journal* July/Aug. 1992
c. *INFOWORLD*, Aug. 24 1992
d. Doll & Associates Report, 1992
e. Doll & Associates Report, 1992
f. *Computer World*, Aug. 10, 1992
g. *Information Week*, July 20, 1992
h. *Information Week*, July 20, 1992
i. *Computer World*, Aug. 10, 1992
j. *Information Week*, Feb. 10, 1992
k. *Computer World*, Feb.13, 1992
l. *Computer World*, April 6, 1992
m. *Information Week*, Feb. 10, 1992
n. *Information Week*, Feb. 10, 1992
o. *Information Week*, June 24, 1992
p. *Computer World*, Aug. 17, 1992
q. *Computer World*, Aug. 17, 1992

Percentage of Mainframe Downsizers

Moving Mainframe Work to:

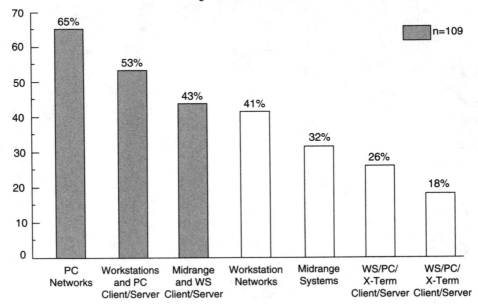

Percentage of Mainframe Downsizers

Aggressively Moving to Open Systems/UNIX

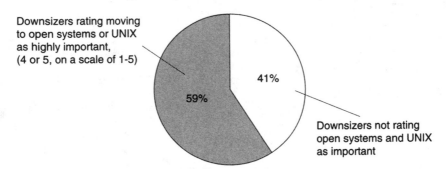

Note: Mainframe downsizers for the purpose of these analyses were defined as respondents rating "moving work off mainframes," on a 5 point scale of importance, at 4 or 5.

Source: Hewlett-Packard Survey, May/June 1993

Figure 1-1: *Target downsizing platforms.*

Many of the operations applications listed could be considered as not only time-critical, but also mission-critical to many companies, i.e., order entry, payroll, distribution, and inventory.

Table 1-2: New Applications Placed on UNIX by Downsizers[a]

Less Time-critical (Decision Support)	More Time-critical (Operations)	Unclear
Database (Oracle)	Order entry	Enhancements
CASE and management tools	Payroll, general ledger	Everything
Ad hoc queries	Inventory tracking, OSHA	Strategic applications
Decision applications	In-store inventory	All applications are potential
Yield management, marketing and sales functionality	Labor scheduling, cash/sales via scan	candidates
Business re-engineering, customer service rather than transactions	Order dispatch	General purpose
	Procurement	Interfaces
Research application	Accounts receivable/ accounts payable	Unknown
Financials, property planning	Sales management	
Executive decision support	Distribution	
Programming language	Dock/yard control	
Manufacturing applications and business data	Marketing	
	Credit	
	Telemarketing	
	Manufacturing/financials	

a.   Source: Responses to Work-Group Technology Survey (1992); categorized by author.

Time-sensitive commercial roles are new for UNIX. Early experimenters with commercial UNIX technology found it deficient in areas assumed fundamental for commercial use, such as data integrity, security, transaction processing management, and automatic backup. Because of these weaknesses, UNIX workstations made their commercial debut where UNIX engineering environment strengths could be leveraged, such as securities trading departments (which have similar team computing demands as highly integrated engineering development teams) or decision support systems (demanding spreadsheet compute power, another engineering requirement).

In addition to being slowed by a lack of commercial robustness, the UNIX commercial cause was set back even further by bad publicity from the "UNIX Wars." The UNIX Wars were instigated by the signing of a cooperative agreement between Sun Microsystems and AT&T in 1987. This agreement was viewed by other hardware vendors as an attempt to control the destiny of UNIX, the only operating system believed to have a chance of becoming truly multi-vendor. The following year, mutual competitors HP, IBM, and DEC (along with several other vendors) joined forces to create another UNIX partnership entitled the Open Software Foundation (OSF) to counterbalance the AT&T/Sun initiative. OSF used the combined market clout of its member companies to foil the AT&T/Sun attempt at UNIX control, and persuade AT&T to place UNIX in the public domain.

The UNIX Wars ended in 1990 with a whimper, and without proclaimed winners or losers. AT&T's UNIX Systems Organization was spun off as UNIX Systems Lab (USL), and is still seen as setting the direction for UNIX kernels today. (USL was recently acquired by Novell, the leading shareholder in the local area network (LAN) market.) Both camps claimed that there really wasn't much to fight about since the two UNIX operating systems were similar enough to allow for relative ease of portability and interoperability versus alternatives in the proprietary world.

The sparring vendors realized that fighting over UNIX was doing the UNIX cause more harm than good. Their brawl made the world painfully aware that multiple flavors of UNIX kernels exist. MIS managers began to see the UNIX operating systems as simply another set of proprietary platforms. Many decided to wait until the confusion let up before giving UNIX a try. The damage stretched as far away as Japan. When Japanese MIS managers were asked by HP in the previously mentioned 1992 survey about the potential for UNIX penetration in commercial applications, many mentioned the separation of UNIX worlds as a major inhibitor.

Fortunately, significant progress has been made since 1990 toward uniting UNIX camps. USL and OSF have now completed a phase of rapprochement. USL announced support for OSF's Distributed Computing Environment (DCE) technology in their 1993 operating system, and now, six of the competing UNIX vendors, Hewlett-Packard, IBM, The Santa Cruz Operation, SunSoft, Univel, and UNIX Systems Laboratories, Inc. have announced what they call, "a Common Open Software Environment (COSE), which will provide standard components for a common desktop environment, networking, graphics, multimedia, object technology, and systems management that can run on top of the UNIX kernels of any developer that supports it," *PC Week* March 22, 1993).

The commercial robustness of UNIX has also come a long way. Larry DeBoever, a well-known downsizing consultant based in Connecticut, believes the prior deficiencies of UNIX are to be "completely fixed" with recent USL UNIX releases.

For many U.S. MIS managers today, the dust has cleared on the question of commercial UNIX feasibility. UNIX has joined the list of viable commercial operating systems options. Soon MIS managers who claim UNIX is not commercially robust will risk being labeled as uninformed. This is good news for Japanese MIS managers trying to break away from excessive dependence on mainframe operating systems. The proprietary shackles may be coming off at last. The UNIX market, according to InfoCorp, has grown at a 20% annual clip from 1990, to exceed $30 billion in 1992.

W. Connor, an experienced downsizing CIO from Motorola, the worldwide semiconductor and electronic equipment manufacturer, goes so far as to claim that there are "virtually no applications in Motorola's business that should NOT be taken off the mainframe and placed on a UNIX platform." This opinion has been generally substantiated by the accounts of downsizing MIS managers interviewed for this book. The following sections document their stories in detail. MIS managers now in the process of considering their downsizing options, should find these stories useful references.

Mainframe Vendors Fight Back

With such clouds on the horizon for mainframe market growth, it is no wonder that IBM is scrambling to shift its enormous organizational weight away from its heretofore bread-and-butter mainframe business toward the higher growth open systems/client server market. It is also little surprise that IBM and other mainframe vendors are also trying to discourage installed customers from downsizing. Their main tactic is to play up the natural anxiety IBM mainframe customers have concerning moving to the relatively new world of open systems. 23.7% of mainframe owners surveyed recently by Network World, a publisher of Computing Journals, claim that vendors have tried to dissuade them from moving to newer downsized paradigms. Most pointed fingers at their hardware vendor and complained that the vendor had generated FUD (Fear, Uncertainty, and Doubt). One even accused his vendor of "trying to discredit me, trying to get my clients to fire me."

An IBM shop MIS director recounted a confusing IBM experience to the Network World researchers. Apparently he had been seriously considering downsizing to a UNIX client/server topology, but could not get his IBM sales representative to provide recommendations on how to proceed. Instead he heard only about the weaknesses of early UNIX systems. He then asked to speak with representatives from IBM's RS6000 UNIX organization. The RS6000 sales team arrived and promoted the benefits of UNIX as if they were from a completely different company.

IBM's recent reorganization into independent lines of business indicates that its management team also recognizes that IBM is truly made up of several different companies. Customers are beginning to wonder, however, how to build client/server systems populated with products from several, sometimes competing, and often incompatible, IBM company systems.

On the other side of the downsizing fence, we find hardware and software vendors pushing the technology edge with UNIX downsizing and client/server products and solutions. Early downsizing companies were faced with the daunting task of developing their own network and system management tools. Some went as far as hard coding transaction monitoring functionality into TCP/IP (more details on UNIX transaction monitoring in Chapter 6). Others went without many of the system management capabilities deemed essential for operating commercial systems. A handful of these pioneering companies and vendors have banded together under the name MOSES (not the religious saint, but the Major Open Systems Environment Standards group) to identify and make visible downsizing trouble spots that need standard procedures and technology. Mike Prince from the Burlington Coat Factory is one of the founding members.

For a company looking at downsizing today, the choice of capable vehicles is expanding rapidly as new downsizing and client/-server-enabling platforms, tools, and applications are brought to market with breakneck speed. The mainstays of the mainframe software environment, including Computer Associates, Dun & Bradstreet, Lawson Software Inc., SAP AG, Cincom Systems Inc., and Pilot Software Inc., are aggressively moving their applications and tools to UNIX. Relational database vendors, such as Oracle, INFORMIX, Sybase, and Ingres, are adding robustness to their products in the areas of data integrity, security, and networked database functions to mitigate many of the early UNIX weaknesses. Integrated CASE tools from Andersen Consulting and Texas Instruments are being announced which support both client and server development with the same CASE tool repository. Conversion tools for transporting custom CICS Cobol code are already here, and most recently, even IBM announced it is porting IBM's CICS transaction processing environment to UNIX (both IBM UNIX and HP-UX). These tools and applications are certainly not completely fool-proof solutions. They represent, however, an important pool of expertise to which the first downsizing MIS managers did not have access.

You may have noticed among the entries in the list of downsizing stories in the press (Table 1-1) that more and more companies have gained the courage to go all the way with downsizing and actually pull the plug on their mainframes. *Information Week's* February 1992 issue describes how TRW Inc.'s corporate IS department shifted all their corporate applications to a client/server network of midrange servers and PC networks. TRW then lugged their IBM 4381 mainframe out the door as part of a program providing annual savings of $10 million. Another company, Georgia-Pacific, is described in the same article as selling their two IBM 4300s for scrap metal. Apparently all they could get for each of the mainframes was $6000. That was "only enough to purchase a new PC client," according to Georgia-Pacific's MIS director.

The downsizing road to client/server is certainly not completely smooth yet, but the road crew is out there paving it with tremendous energy. A description of the most effective downsizing platforms and tools is included in Chapters 5 and 6 of this book.

How Long Are Japanese Users Going to Stay on the Sidelines?

Yokogawa Electric Corporation

For most Japanese companies, Yokogawa Electric Corporation's leap to embody a full-fledged, enterprise-wide integrated information system based on client/server architecture is hard to believe. Yokogawa is virtually the first Japanese company to do so. And when they jumped, they went whole hog. The nearly $2 billion test and measurement company is encircling an IBM 3090 mainframe with an entourage of HP-UX UNIX servers equipped with Oracle database and application software. These servers are distributed throughout the major divisions of Yokogawa, from administration and research and development through to engineering systems and sales (Figure 1-2). No one at Yokogawa, however, was cornered into making career-threatening decisions akin to those made by Mike Prince at

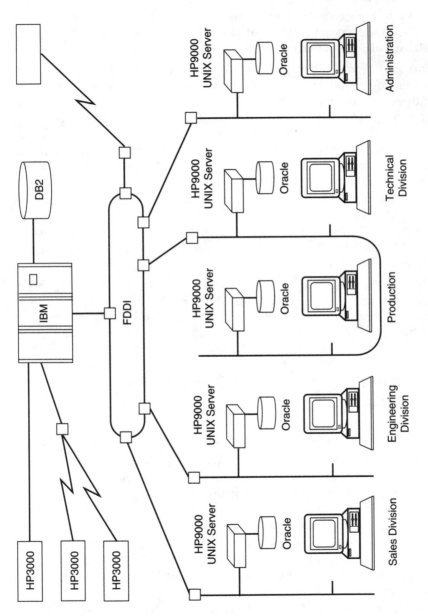

Figure 1-2: *Yokogawa Electric Corporation's downsized system configuration.*

Burlington Coat Factory. No, Murakami-san, Yokogawa's strategic information systems chief, was seen as constructing and implementing prudent information system development plans and proposals based on hard facts and clear logic.

Yokogawa's evolution began in the early 1980s when a program was launched for squeezing waste out of manufacturing systems. A task force of engineers and managers, led by Murakami-san, used Toyota's now famous Kanban just-in-time inventory system as a conceptual springboard for resolving the special inventory challenges of smaller lot manufacturing systems typical of Yokogawa's test and measurement industry. The result was NYPS (New Yokogawa Production Productivity Prosperity System) which challenged conventional wisdom on the factory floor by switching from "Front Process Push Production"—produce as much as you can to supply the next step of the production chain—to "Subsequent Process One-at-a-Time Pull Production." The success of NYPS made buffer inventories a thing of the past at Yokogawa.

The NYPS team then focused on improving manufacturing time to market and quickly realized that they were embarking on a much longer journey. The actual production of parts and products (the focus of the original NYPS program) was a mere 2-3 days out of the average 30-day order fulfillment process. The longer process stretched across many organizational boundaries, including parts procurement departments, testing units, logistics, etc. It did not take long to realize that even fixing the all-encompassing order fulfillment process would not be enough to reap the full benefits of the NYPS program. Improvements were necessary along all of Yokogawa's business systems, e.g., engineering, sales, and marketing, making the program a company-wide strategic initiative.

The company-wide charter became a reality during the yen/dollar exchange rate recession of the mid eighties. The management team created a new organization to spearhead what they called "a program for corporate strengthening" and populated it with senior members of the NYPS task force. The new organization was chartered to re-engineer Yokogawa's business process for "meeting the challenges of globalization and recession at home." In contrast to the initial "one point" (in Japanese, ten-teki) NYPS effort, which focused solely on direct manufacturing, the new charter was to take on the full geometric "plane" (in Japanese men-teki). All production-related activities, including sales, were fair game for this project, and all systems solutions (decision support, administration, remote office, and those of affiliates) fell under the jurisdiction of the program team.

The team took this carte blanche and began re-engineering company processes only to find their program stalled by an MIS shop which could not keep up with the flood of system change proposals emanating from their efforts. Average system development cycles took a year or more at Yokogawa, causing serious bottlenecks and threatening to transform the expanded NYPS program from a major change activity to a much less ambitious "business as usual" exercise. The backlog of requests grew sky high and the MIS staff was placed under enormous pressure to perform to impossible schedules given the constraints of their centralized host/terminal environment. Even MIS managers became frustrated enough to spring head-long into exploring IS alternatives for salvaging the program, including mainframe downsizing, although few at Yokogawa were sure at that time what downsizing would really mean.

The winds of change gathered speed when an April 1989 meeting of the board of directors launched a new "Total Company Information System Investigation Group." The organization was nicknamed Z-Pro (for ZenSha or total company) and was chartered with the arduous task of aligning business requirements and information system capabilities throughout the company, to achieve an elusive goal sought after by many companies on both sides of the pacific: a truly strategic information system. Murakami-san was placed in charge of the effort.

Major changes were underway...but wait a second...how do we get from here to where Yokogawa is today, implementing an aggressive transformation to open systems? Why did UNIX come into the picture at all? After all, UNIX was certainly not considered a viable commercial systems option by most Japanese companies in 1990.

UNIX had had a long tradition within Yokogawa's engineering and manufacturing communities, communities from which many of the Z-Pro task force members had come. Moreover, Yokogawa had an extremely close relationship with Hewlett-Packard (HP), the dominant U.S. Commercial RISC/UNIX platform vendor. Yokogawa and HP jointly own a development and distribution company headquartered in the Tokyo area called Yokogawa Hewlett-Packard (YHP), responsible for HP's computer systems and test and measurement offerings in Japan.

Murakami-san also had a close business relationship with the flamboyant Japanese-speaking Bill Totten, founder and president of Ashisuto, an international software distribution company headquartered in Japan. From Mr. Totten, he was able to gain insights into advances made by U.S. third-party software application vendors adding commercial robustness to UNIX. Mr. Totten's sometimes iconoclastic denouncements of mainframe-centered topologies also rubbed off on the Z-Pro team members as they mapped out plans to meet their system design goals of:

- Obtaining necessary data in REAL TIME
- Maximum system response time of 3 SECONDS
- Data integrity 100% GUARANTEED
- 365-day, 24-hour service provision
- NO NEED for manuals

The MIS department at this time was also forced into a major break with the past. Seeds were planted to spin off MIS as an independent systems integrator, and the MIS team was scrambling to build systems development capabilities to ensure a safe landing in their new role. MIS was in fact incorporated as a separate company in 1990, one year following the creation of Z-Pro. With the spin-off impending, Z-Pro took on a whole new meaning to the MIS team. It became their proving ground, for convincing both current and future Yokogawa and non-Yokogawa clientele of their leading edge systems development capabilities.

Just as the Z-Pro team started their inquiry, UNIX was starting to be viewed as a viable commercial operating system in the U.S. Several Yokogawa departments had also broken ground with early UNIX systems in commercial applications. One fairly large sales division had, in fact, successfully implemented a prototype sales support system using UNIX and Oracle relational database software to link up numerous remote sales offices.

With this backdrop, numerous organizational and management vectors were aligned for implementing a full-fledged open system downsizing solution. Z-Pro's list of system requirements for meeting their design goals were:

- Use open systems
- Downsize completely
- Use Relational Database Management Systems (RDBMS)
- Construct a LAN infrastructure
- Align and integrate systems throughout the company
- Aggressively promote End-User Computing (EUC)

Even with all the momentum building for open systems, the team harbored doubts about the applicability of UNIX to all types of commercial computing. They were comfortable with using UNIX with the less urgent information-intensive applications (in Japanese,

Johokei), but were less certain about UNIX integrity and reliability for transaction-intensive and time-sensitive order entry processes. As Yokogawa managers currently go about installing new systems, they rate UNIX as 70% okay for these more demanding tasks. The managers expect to retain their mainframe indefinitely as a company-wide database server, even after all Yokogawa's applications are moved to UNIX.

Murakami-san sees the current program as the natural result of ten years of accumulated accomplishments achieved by various Yokogawa task forces, many of which he headed. He took a moment during a recent interview to reflect on the rows of green pine trees neatly maintained around Yokogawa's Tokyo headquarters, an environment where such trees can only survive if they are an important priority in the company's culture. Murakami-san comments "Shozo Yokogawa (Yokogawa's founder and chairman) built many businesses with the patience of a Japanese gardener. These trees are a refreshing reminder of that philosophy. Z-Pro has been well nurtured by the management team. Hopefully it will grow into a tree of gold."

Is Downsizing Really Transferable to Japan?

Articles in the press often take up the subject of how different Japan is from the rest of the world. Many pages have been allocated to discussing how Japanese have unique management practices, social mores, and views on life. The common Japanese explanation for these differences is that Japan is an island country "Shima Guni" never conquered by the marauding Mongols and other mainland people responsible for churning the ethnic pool on the Asian continent. In fact, the only time when Japan was close to being conquered was when Khublai Khan attacked two times by sea between 1266 and 1294. Both times the Mongol forces were driven back by ferocious wind storms, often referred to by the Japanese as "KamiKaze" or divine wind. Some unique features of the Japanese computer environment are also worth noting.

IBM's Technology without IBM's Dominance

Few would dispute that the fountain of technology for Japan's computer industry has been IBM. IBM established a fully owned Japanese subsidiary in the early 1960s with special permission from the Japanese government and proceeded to build the Japanese computer market from scratch, much in the way IBM gave birth to computer markets around the globe. IBM Japan's organization, however, met with a unique Japanese response. Fiercely competitive local electronics firms, well versed in learning and leveraging foreign technologies, sprung out of nowhere to challenge IBM's lead. Japan is the only western country in which IBM is not the dominant player. IBM, with less than 16% share of the overall Japanese computer market, according to 1991 Dataquest estimates, has now fallen behind Fujitsu, Hitachi and/or NEC in selling into most Japanese industries.

IBM's relative weakness in Japan can also be partially explained by Japanese government protectionism starting in the late 1960s. A recent study completed by Bain & Company, a major U.S. management consulting firm, reports that non-Japanese computer vendor share of the private sector in 1965 was 70%, and only 38% of the corresponding public sector. Non-Japanese vendor share subsequently declined in both sectors, but the decline was much sharper in the public sector. By 1975, share of the private sector had dropped to close to 50%, while the public sector share plummeted to near 8%. The lockout in the public sector has continued until today. According to the study, public sector share still remains a low 8%.

MITI is reported to have been quite open about their protectionist intentions in 1975, when they asked all government agencies to do their bit to ensure that consolidated sales of non-Japanese computer vendors did not exceed the 50% market share line. Government agencies apparently heeded the call. A listing of major Japanese government computer purchases during the mid 1980s, compiled and published in Utsumi Ichiro's 1989 book, *The Computer Industry Three Years from Today,* reveals that of 19 Japanese government agency purchases, only two included non-Japanese equipment.

Today, IBM's weakest Japan market remains the government sector. This may, however, change significantly with a 1992 U.S./Japan trade negotiation agreement. MITI has agreed to now actively promote (!) Japanese government purchases of U.S. computer products in the years to come.

IBM managers did not take Japanese protectionism without resistance. They chose, however, to strike back in an arena more favorably disposed to their cause. IBM lashed out in U.S. courts against both Fujitsu and Hitachi in the early 1980s claiming infringement of intellectual property rights. Both cases were settled out of court, but the legitimacy of IBM's complaints regarding intellectual property were generally recognized as valid. After all, what other company has contributed so much to computer technology as it is known today in Japan?

One manifestation of IBM's Japanese legacy is the numerous English terms (usually written in Japanese phonetics) populating Japanese operating and training manuals. An MIS manager interviewed in the early 1980s by this author once winked knowingly when the subject came up and remarked, "You would be surprised by the similarity between IBM and Fujitsu operating systems, whole parts appear to have been copied verbatim."

Beyond having common IBM technology roots, similarities between U.S. and Japanese computer industries are difficult to find. These two countries have followed different paths in the way they develop, sell, and use information systems. For starters, the Japanese computer industry is remarkably devoid of Independent Software Vendors (ISVs).

Where Are the ISVs?

One distinguishing factor of the Japanese computer industry is the scarcity of packaged software, and the ISVs that churn them out. The operating system for PCs in Japan came originally from U.S.-based Microsoft Corp., and each hardware vendor has tweaked it to create their own proprietary Japanese version. Not to say that there aren't any big Japanese names in PC software. Just Systems, for instance, is a Japanese company noted for developing a word processing package called "Ichitaro" used by over 90% of Japanese PC owners. It is in the development of software applications for larger platforms (mainframe and midrange systems) that the Japanese have apparently run into insurmountable barriers. There are virtually no best-selling Japanese (or even non-Japanese) mainframe and midrange software packages. Customers, for the most part, subcontract application software development, put together homegrown solutions, or have their hardware vendors slap together semi-custom software out of proprietary software modules. Software houses play a more subservient role in the Japanese market. Hardware vendors and large companies see them as a source of inexpensive programming help—a far cry from the posture taken by their dynamic U.S. counterparts.

Those familiar with the U.S. computer market are keenly aware of how ISVs have taken a leadership role in shaping the U.S. industry. Few could imagine the history of PCs without Microsoft, spreadsheets without Visicalc and Lotus, MRP without ASK, process cell control without Allen Bradley, financials without Dun & Bradstreet, and mainframe utilities without Computer Associates. Breakthroughs in today's market are also often generated by ISV talent. Data is much more accessible today thanks to relational database technology from Sequel/Sybase, Oracle, INFORMIX, and Ingres (all ISVs), and computers can now be linked together more effectively due to PC network operating systems from Microsoft and Novell.

Japanese systems integrators also exhibit a much more subservient posture than their U.S. counterparts. Japan has only a small group of system integrators who can be legitimately classified as both competent and independent, according to MITI's Department for the Promotion of Information Processing. Most Japanese systems integration is done by internal MIS teams of major corporations, closely affiliated software houses, or hardware vendors. Andersen Consulting has been the most successful U.S. firm trying to create a Japanese systems integration market. EDS has just broken ground in Tokyo. EDS managers are currently refining their development tools for Japanese use, and aggressively recruiting and training Japanese staff. Oddly, the $47 billion Japanese computer market is nearly half the size of the U.S., but both the software and systems integration industries languish in an embryonic state.

Why does it matter that Japan has few ISVs and system integrators? Let's first go back to U.S. MIS managers and ask what ISVs mean to them. Thanks to ISVs and system integrators, U.S. MIS managers are not trapped into accepting every proposal pitched by their hardware vendors. When in doubt, they can call on friendly ISVs or independent system integrators, known for their broad-based experience with a variety of hardware platforms, and obtain additional perspectives on alternative solutions. With the dawning of the U.S. open systems market, MIS managers also have gained the freedom to plug and play multiple platforms, and have come to regard system integrators as perhaps the most knowledgeable experts on how to put it all together. This is not to say that many U.S. MIS managers don't also feel locked in by U.S. proprietary platforms, many do. But at least they have escape hatches today, many more routes of escape than their Japanese counterparts, stuck in the cross fire of warring proprietary system empires in Japan.

From the perspective of the Japanese market, the power that U.S. ISVs wield vis-a-vis U.S. hardware vendors is astounding. IBM's turf battles with Microsoft are a good example. Microsoft, the developer of DOS (the standard operating system for IBM and IBM-compatible PCs around the world), had agreed to jointly develop and market with IBM an operating system called OS/2. OS/2 was promised to be the next generation multi-tasking, 32-bit, object-oriented operating system for the desktop. Several years into the OS/2 development program it became increasingly apparent that Microsoft managers had their own agenda. They released their own "Windows" software containing many of the preliminary OS/2 improvements and took the market by storm. IBM and Microsoft exchanged harsh words and threatened legal action, but neither party blinked. They have now parted ways to fight it out in the next generation of operating systems, those based on object-oriented technologies.

Typical of the competitive dynamism found in the U.S. software industry, IBM and Microsoft are not nearly alone in the new arena of next generation operating systems. At least six viable ISV and hardware vendor contenders are stepping up to the bar. The Santa Cruz Operation (ISV) is ready with a PC UNIX "Open Desktop" platform, Novell and UNIX Systems Lab (ISVs) are launching a "Univel" UNIX networking platform, Sun (hardware vendor) is counting on expanding territory with a commercial desktop version of Sun's "Solaris" UNIX operating system, Steve Job's Next Inc. (hardware vendor) is promoting a platform considered the most technically advanced today, "NextStep," Microsoft (ISV) is vigorously promoting a semi-object-oriented operating system called "Windows NT," to be introduced in July 1993 (to be enhanced later with more object technology resulting from a project called Cairo), and the joint venture of two previous archrivals in the PC industry, IBM and Apple (hardware vendors), is bringing to market yet another flavor of object-oriented operating system, developed by some of Apple's best engineers.

The success of U.S. ISVs, and the hard times upon which many U.S. hardware vendors have fallen has led some informed observers to recommend that the U.S. call it quits in the hardware industry. A highly influential *Harvard Business Review* article written by Andrew S. Rappaport and Shmuel Halevi, entitled "The Computerless Computer Company," questions the viability of sustainable profitability in the U.S. hardware business. "By the year 2000," the article states, "the most successful computer companies will be those that buy computers rather than build them...The future belongs to the computerless computer company."[1]

---

1. Rappaport, Andrew S. and Halevi, Shmuel, "The Computerless Computer Company," *Harvard Business Review*, Jul.–Aug. 1991, 69–80.

It is no wonder that Japan's Ministry of International Trade and Industry (MITI) issued a "Year 2000 Vision" for the Information Processing Industry, containing a stern message to Japan's software houses. The message: Japan will never be competitive in the computer business on a global scale if Japanese software houses do not strive to build application package development skills and system integration capabilities equivalent to their western counterparts. This is not the first time MITI has tried to revamp the Japanese world of software and system integration. Special tax incentives were provided in a MITI "Sigma" program to nurture the development of this nascent industry. The record so far, however, has not been as positive as MITI would have liked. MITI managers admit that only a handful of Japanese software houses can hold their own in true systems integration projects, and fewer have mastered the business of developing successful software application packages. Why is this?

Conventional wisdom in Japan says that Japanese have a cultural aversion to application packages similar to their distaste for second-hand goods (which are also very difficult to find in that country). MIS managers say they do not believe software developed for another company could possibly meet their needs. A major Japanese Insurance Company MIS manager mentioned during a recent interview that he had once been approached by a sales representative from Digital Equipment Corporation (DEC). To his surprise the DEC salesperson could show him a software package for every computing need he could imagine. In the end, however, he reluctantly turned the DEC salesperson away. His explanation: "All those packages may have worked...but somehow...I couldn't believe that a vendor promoting so many packages would put in the extra effort to help us adjust the software to truly meet our needs."

Two other impediments to the emergence of Japanese ISVs are:

- Greater fragmentation of the computer industry
- Lack of a nurturing venture capital environment, similar to that enjoyed in the U.S., especially in Silicon Valley

Fragmented? Fragmented in what sense? Japan's computer industry differs from the rest of the world in that it is NOT dominated by IBM. In the U.S., IBM's $32 billion of revenues tower over all its U.S. competitors. The second and third largest, DEC and HP, have 1991 U.S. revenues of $4-5 billion each, less than 1/6 IBM's size. As mentioned earlier, IBM's share of the Japan market, however, has been only a moderate 15-20% in recent years, and shrinking over time.

The massive volumes of IBM's U.S.-installed customer base opened expanding vistas of promising revenues to would-be ISVs considering launching their first packages on IBM platforms at the dawning of the U.S. application software industry. Opportunities for Japanese ISVs paled in comparison. Japan's market pie is sliced too many ways by too many proprietary vendors.

Japanese software houses aggressive enough to throw their hats in the ring and give application software a try, found it difficult to get financial backing for the many person-years required to produce packages of the caliber found in the U.S. Silicon Valley's entrepreneur-nurturing venture capital community has no counterpart in Japan. Unable to obtain funds for developing packages from scratch, some Japanese software houses tried to convert custom packages created for one customer into more generalized versions for subsequent sale, only to find few interested customers. The converted packages had too many idiosyncratic bells and whistles incorporated at the behest of the original customer.

A moderate -sized Japanese software developer recognized by MITI as one of the more competent providers of system integration services, decided to try and break into the package software market a couple of years ago. Instead of giving the original customer full rights to a futures trading solution developed under contract, the software house managers kept the rights and in return, gave the customer a sizable discount. To their dismay, however, few companies could use the package without considerable rework. Apparently, many of the components had been written in a language unique to the first company's environment. The incompatible code still languishes with few customers to be found. A senior director at the software house says he will be lucky if he makes a profit on his application software experiment.

But why is it so hard to get the ISV industry started? Independent software houses have grown up in such numbers and exhibited such staying power and vitality in the U.S., it is hard to believe that a computer industry could exist without them—they almost seem like natural inhabitants of the information system landscape. On close inspection, however, the challenges involved in moving from the typical Japanese software house business, subcontracting of software development labor (contract programming), to the risk-taking environment of software package investment, is not so simple.

The SW House Contract Programming Straitjacket

Simply put, application software managers are investors, and contract programmers are labor bosses. The management mentality of these two industries is worlds apart. What makes typical contract programming managers tick? Profits in their business are achieved by maximizing the charge per programming hour (revenue) and minimizing programmer salary and benefits (costs). The hourly charge for typical programming services is difficult to control due to competition from other contract programmers, but managers can do something about the average programming salary in their own shops. They can hire younger inexpensive programmers, and invest little in training and productivity tools. As the programmers age and expect higher wages, the managers can encourage them to leave and create their own small software "body shops," to keep the age mix in their own shops young and inexpensive. Currently there are more than 10,000 shops like this in Japan. To keep programmers fully occupied, contract programming managers avoid reusing code, thereby maximizing time spent programming, and thus, billable hours. Managers really earned their keep when they successfully attach themselves to a major customer by developing mission-critical program code. They are thereby locked in for years of guaranteed work supporting and revising the custom software, simply because no one else knows the code. After a while, the customers realize their overdependence on the software house, and embrace it with an equity investment to avoid having it fail. The software house now has a permanent home...what bliss!

By contrast, profits to the managers of an application software package developer are revenue (price and number of packages sold) minus development cost (person-years to develop). This formula drives them to a completely different set of behaviors. They hire and train the most productive software developers (regardless of tenure), use the most powerful languages and development tools, maximize the reusability of code, and minimize the need for software support (excess support requirements are a drain, not a boon, to the application package developer).

Moving from the labor-intensive world of contract programming to the investment-intensive world of application packages is certainly not business as usual. How many managers can go through this type of personality change without being spurred to it by the market opportunities and nurturing capital environments of the U.S.? MITI's frustration with the task of motivating Japanese software houses to aspire to the greater heights of software application development is quite understandable.

The contract programming mentality also drives software houses to become highly dependent on one particular hardware vendor's platform. Most software houses are small enough to get by with just a few large customers. Choosing customers with the same platform saves training investment.

Japanese Value Added Resellers (purveyors of bundled hardware and software solutions, VARs) also depend excessively upon a single vendor. Many provide contract programming services along with their hardware and so take on a contract programming mentality. Moreover, their sales leads come mostly from the hardware vendor (that's where customers generally feel most comfortable calling), and service revenue (and profits) are, for the most part, circumscribed by VAR/Vendor agreements. Straying to support another vendor's platform is not only expensive (learning to sell and support another proprietary platform is no easy task), it can be dangerous. Less loyal VARs can suddenly find themselves without the vendor sales leads and in some cases, without service rights. Major hardware vendors can virtually pull the plug on a VAR's business, if they so desire.

Why Customers Only Talk to Their Mainframe Vendors

Without an independent software and systems integration industry, Japanese MIS managers have few places to go for advice and services besides their mainframe vendors. Nervous about the large budget applied to information systems, MIS managers look to minimize their financial risk by ensuring their vendor has the deepest pockets and the most trustworthy sales representatives, sales representatives who are ready to help out if anything goes wrong. "Trustworthy Sales Reps" has ranked high as a buying factor in Nikkei's well-subscribed computer purchasing surveys for many years in a row. The MIS manager's need to reduce technology risk also brings him closer to the hardware vendor. Since all platforms are proprietary, only the mainframe vendor knows the current and future details of the platform design. Even VARs considered to be members of the inside circle of a hardware vendor's group of closely affiliated third parties, have trouble providing expertise at a level satisfactory to many MIS managers. All this adds up to excessive MIS dependence on Japanese mainframe hardware vendors for both hardware and software solutions. According to Inteco Research, mainframe-related expenditures made up 41.9% of the 1989 Japanese market versus only 23.5% of the U.S.

This greater control that mainframe vendors exercise over Japanese customer IT and system design strategies may have also contributed to another unique characteristic of the Japanese market: Japanese midrange systems are different. Midrange systems in the U.S. are generally interconnectible, scalable, and often run numerous applications supporting multiple business functions. By contrast, Japanese midrange systems are called Office Computers (Ofcon in Japanese) and are generally operated as stand-alone turnkey solutions dedicated to a limited set of functions. DEC and HP's U.S. midrange systems of the 70s and 80s worked in powerful clusters and took on much of the computing burden of smaller mainframes, especially those installed in individual departments of larger corporations, and the MIS shops of medium and smaller size companies. U.S. midrange systems met with such commercial and engineering customer enthusiasm that HP and DEC quickly mushroomed into sizable enough vendors to challenge IBM in major accounts. Neither DEC nor HP have achieved proportionate shares of the Japanese market, even when measured as a percentage of IBM's Japanese market share. Japan's Ofcon market is instead dominated by products from mainframe vendors (Fujitsu, NEC, IBM). Even IBM's AS/400 (typically known as a midrange system in the U.S.) has been marketed in Japan as a stand-alone turnkey Ofcon system.

Is it possible that Japanese mainframe vendors positioned midrange computers on distant and separate turf to avoid eroding their more profitable mainframe business? Once successful in positioning midrange systems as non-threatening Ofcon systems, Japanese vendors then built the Ofcon market with a vengeance. The dramatic growth of the Ofcon market helped fuel overall market growth for Japan's computer industry during the late 1980s. This segment is now an $8 billion market, representing almost 17% of the industry. Japanese customers, however, are left holding the bag. Thanks to Ofcon, Japan companies today are even more populated by isolated islands of computing than their U.S. counterparts. Japanese MIS managers are yelling out in customer surveys for UNIX networking capabilities to connect these Ofcon islands.

Where Are the PC LANs?

The PC LANs, which are connecting desktop PCs in the U.S. and spreading like wildfire, are difficult to find in Japan. The numerous flavors of Japanese MS-DOS operating systems (mentioned earlier) add significantly to the complexity of PC connectivity, and may have inhibited the spread of PC LANs. Nevertheless, proprietary DOS operating systems do not deserve all of the blame. Lower penetration of PCs in the Japanese office may also be responsible for the slow start.

Behind low PC penetration is the complexity of the Japanese language. Few Japanese managers have been willing to take on the challenge of learning Kanji Henkan (the Japanese method for typing ideographs using phonetics). In addition, more senior managers are prone to shun the keyboard, preferring to demonstrate their prowess in Japanese calligraphy, acquired over the years of painstakingly penning Japanese business memos and correspondence.

This is changing rapidly as younger Japanese find it easier to type memos than raise their expertise in calligraphy to an acceptable level. Many more PCs (and now PC laptops) are finding their way onto crowded Japanese desks, and LAN technology is making a beachhead with localized products from Novell and LAN Manager. Industry experts are projecting an inflection growth point for the Japanese PC LAN market in 1993. PC LAN penetration in 1991 however, is estimated to be still under 1% of Japanese PCs. A substantial portion of the PCs which are linked in Japan happen to be Apple Macintoshes.

Given All the Inhibitors, How Can Japan Downsize?

HP surveyed 300 Japanese MIS managers in 1991 and another 400 in 1992 to identify emerging trends in the unique Japan environment. As expected, the surveys revealed a rising interest in commercial UNIX, but few HP managers expected to see the virtual landslide of Japanese customers aggressively moving applications off their mainframes to less expensive midrange, workstation, and PC alternatives. Greater than 50% of responding companies ranked the importance of making the move at 4 or 5, on a scale of 1 to 5. The 1991 respondents estimated their average investments in mainframes to be 53% of their total information systems budget, and projected a slight decline in this percentage to 51% two years out, after which their responses indicated a significant drop to 43% five years from the date of the survey. 1992 respondents answering the same question projected a precipitous drop in their mainframe investments from 51% to 45%, only two years out! Behind this sudden shift away from mainframes is an equally sudden shift of the Japanese economy into recession. Japan's stock market dropped by a steep 30% early in 1992, seriously undermining consumer confidence, and slipping the country into a troublesome recession from which it has yet to recover.

Along with a substantial shaving of Japanese capital equipment spending, pressure is being applied to IS budgets as well. It is probably more than coincidence that the sector hardest hit by the recession, manufacturing, shows the highest interest, according to the 1992 HP survey, in moving to downsized client/server configurations.

The survey also indicates that the number of MIS managers who emphasize open systems, downsizing, and UNIX when purchasing Ofcons, will double over the next two years. The role of Ofcons is changing in their minds from being "turnkey" to "network server," as they chart out their journey off the mainframe.

Where Are the Mainframe Vendors in All of This?

Mainframe vendors are approaching the downsizing fad in very much the same way as they managed the midrange systems challenge by creating Ofcons. Each is defining downsizing in a way that best meets their business needs. To some, connecting PCs to the mainframe instead of dumb terminals is a form of downsized client/-server computing (with the obvious benefit to the vendor of leaving the mainframe intact). Mainframe vendors with strong workstation offerings, emphasize the benefits of workstations as clients on the network. Almost all claim that the fruits of downsizing and client/-server can be relished without moving to UNIX (proprietary operating systems provide these vendors with higher profit margins).

According to the HP survey, many Japanese MIS managers have been persuaded by their mainframe vendors that the vendors are well-equipped to take care of their downsizing needs, if not right away, sometime in the future. Perhaps "downsizing," like "midrange," is being defined by Japanese vendors using a different spin. It is interesting that these customers give the same vendors low scores on operating cost and open systems capabilities, factors considered critical to downsizing by many of their U.S. counterparts. It is also ironic that the mainframe vendor boasting the largest number of customers

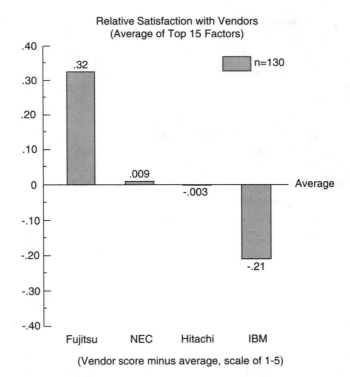

Relative Satisfaction with Vendors
(Average of Top 15 Factors)

n=130

.32
.009
-.003
-.21

Fujitsu   NEC   Hitachi   IBM

(Vendor score minus average, scale of 1-5)

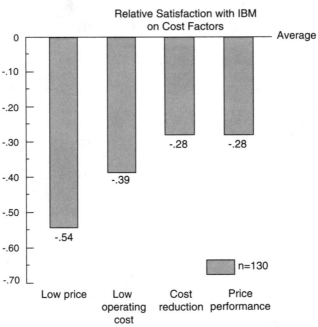

Relative Satisfaction with IBM
on Cost Factors

Average

-.28   -.28
-.39
-.54

n=130

Low price   Low   Cost   Price
             operating reduction performance
             cost

(IBM score minus average, scale of 1-5)

Source: Hewlett-Packard Research 1992

Figure 1-3: *Relative customer satisfaction with IBM in Japan.*

wanting to move to client/server, Japan IBM, also receives the lowest satisfaction scores on all cost-related factors, including operating cost, price, and price performance (Figure 1-3). The more the Japanese learn about the benefits U.S. MIS managers have realized by downsizing, the less likely they are to quietly follow the carefully laid mainframe-centric plans of their mainframe vendors. This book is one vehicle for learning about such U.S. experiences.

Once Japanese customers achieve greater independence in their system decisions, this independence is likely to spill over to Japanese system integrators and software houses. A handful of these companies, including Nomura Research, Toyo Joho Systems (TIS), Nihon Denshi Keisan (JIPs), ARGOTechno21 Corporation, System Consultants, Sumitomo Electric, SOPIA, and International Systems Service (ISS) have already bucked the traditional system of excessive hardware vendor dependence and developed enough in-house expertise to lead the movement toward multivendor platform solutions. Recently a leading edge Japanese systems integrator was asked by a major Japanese oil company to provide a counter proposal to Fujitsu, the oil company's long term mainframe vendor, on downsizing their mainframes. The oil company apparently did not feel comfortable with Fujitsu's proposal recommending continued mainframe investments.

The Economics
Behind Downsizing

The Savings Are There, Even if They Are Often Difficult to Quantify

From the list of downsizing companies reported in the press and the short descriptions of their accomplishments (Table 1-1), it is clear that the economic benefits of downsizing are real for many companies. It is not uncommon for a company to reduce its IS expense by more than a million dollars by pulling the plug on its mainframe. But why is there so little data on exactly how much you can save, and how it will pan out over time?

Mainframe downsizing is such a new phenomenon that few companies have gone through the full experience, and even fewer have been able to track their costs with sufficient granularity to give a full breakdown, including both the "hard" factors, such as fully negotiated hardware and software prices by system components, and the "soft" factors, such as software development productivity and system management costs, for both MIS and the user community.

Doll & Associates, an Ohio-based information technology consulting firm, has studied two downsizing companies in detail to "describe and explore a phenomenon (downsizing) that is not well understood and to verify cost savings." They chose two companies that had reported significant savings from downsizing, CBS/FOX Video and American Sterilizer.

CBS/FOX Video moved from IBM mainframes to a distributed computing topology and had reportedly reduced their $5.2 million annual MIS budget to $800,000, an astounding reduction of 85%. Doll & Associates came in to verify the savings and found that some of the savings were not directly attributable to mainframe downsizing because they were the result of organizational changes carried out before the downsizing project began. The largest non-attributable portion was a nearly $3 million annual savings derived from selling the manufacturing operations, and thereby lowering MIS costs from $5.8 to $2.8 million. Nevertheless, the verified additional savings from downsizing were significant. The $2.8 million budget was reduced to $800,000 (71%) by unplugging the mainframe.

Doll & Associates believes that the loose coupling of CBS/FOX Video's order processing and general accounting applications for their consumer products and financial functions made downsizing easier and the savings greater for them. Each application could be moved down in relative isolation, and run on low-power PC LAN/server configurations. Concern over the control and auditability of the microcomputer-based applications, sometimes an obstacle to downsizing at other companies, was dispelled when the company's accountants (Coopers & Lybrand) thoroughly tested the downsized applications and reported "adequate levels of control and auditability through system features, assuming strong user control." With consensus achieved, CBS/FOX Video moved full speed ahead to successfully install the new applications and unplug their mainframes over a nine-month period in 1989.

A Doll & Associates study of American Sterilizer confirmed that similar levels of MIS savings were also achieved at the U.S.-based hospital equipment company. Starting with a pilot program in early 1986, American Sterilizer offloaded accounting and manufacturing applications from IBM 4341 and IBM 4381 mainframes to run on PC networks across the company. The cost reductions were dramatic. A $1.6 million MIS budget in 1985 was reduced to $874,000 in 1988, and at the time of the study, was projected to fall to $300,000 in 1990. These figures, however, should be treated with some caution. Doll & Associates comments that depreciation expenses for 700 PCs (which can be a major expense) was not included in the 1988 and 1990 budgets. They also add to the other side of the equation by mentioning that "upgrade cost avoidance" calculations also were not included. Apparently, American Sterilizer would have had to upgrade their mainframe to achieve a functionality and response time equivalent to the downsized system at a cost of $500,000 per year. No matter how the cases are cut, it is clear that moving off mainframes to microcomputer-based topologies has provided these companies with tremendous cost reductions.

Many of these cost savings are being generated by the unprecedented increase in price performance achieved by microprocessor-based computing platforms over the last few years. HP, for instance, has been attaining sustainable price performance increments of 60-70%, and that rate is expected to increase. HP's recent high-end Emerald platform, introduced in early 1992, packed the transaction processing power of a mid- to high-end IBM 3090 mainframe into a compact box 1/8 the size, using 1/8 as much power, and costing 1/3 as much to service. The CPU (Central Processing Unit) cost was 1/10 that of the mainframe. When all peripherals, etc., were attached to complete the configuration, the total savings were calculated to be greater than 5 to 1.

GE Information Services (GEIS), for the most part, agrees with HP's cost reduction estimates. Roger Dyer, GEIS's Manager of Platform Engineering, runs mission-critical applications on both mainframe and HP UNIX server clusters. At the moment he is still hesitant to run his UNIX servers flat out. Yet, even reining them in at 50-75% capacity, he cuts his operating costs significantly versus mainframes. Once he feels confident enough to turn up the gas on the UNIX servers, savings could increase to 5 to 1. More details on GEIS's concerns and achievements are contained in Chapter 6.

Many of the companies interviewed for this book have either achieved or expect to achieve savings of close to 50% from downsizing. This may appear conservative compared to the earlier examples from the press clippings, but perhaps more believable. Even at 50%, however, there have been few times in history where companies have been able to reduce the costs of a critical business function by so much, and at the same time dramatically improve its functionality.

Downsizing economies are difficult to quantify for the largest companies. Generally MIS departments are so vast and the shared costs among departments are so significant that it is difficult to isolate prior and subsequent costs of a particular downsizing project for accurate comparison. More often than not, these companies are also implementing a move to client/server topologies—topologies including Graphical User Interfaces (GUIs) for improving user productivity. Full-fledged client/server implementations can lead to increased (rather than decreased) overall distributed system costs as relatively inexpensive dumb terminals are replaced by intelligent desktop devices throughout the company. These types of programs are often not justifiable through MIS savings, and usually don't need to be. MIS managers champion these programs by developing business cases, demonstrating such expected business benefits as enhanced employee productivity and superior customer service to build management consensus. Other issues surrounding these types of downsizing efforts are discussed in Chapter 7.

Two Case Studies with Real-Life Calculations

Two examples of actual and expected cost reductions for medium-sized downsizing companies have been included here to illustrate the costs savings derived from more straight-forward downsizing programs.

Packaged Food Company

Table 2-1 shows the projected MIS budget for a $500 million packaged food concern operating a typical selection of financial, accounting, order entry, MRP, and inventory management applications. This company is using a third-party application software conversion tool with consulting services to convert all mainframe software to a downsized platform of two medium-sized HP-UX servers connecting PC LANs around the country. During the migration phase in 1992, this company's budget increased because both the mainframe and the distributed system are running in parallel. The one-time costs for migration services provided by the third party (some of which could be considered discretionary) are almost as expensive as the new system itself and are amortized over the four-year period. Even with the migration services included, however, the MIS budget falls to 63% of year one by 1994. If the migration costs are excluded from the budget (bottom of the table), the MIS costs drop to less than 1/2 of year one. The steady-state cost comparison for the mainframe versus the downsized topology (comparative cost for each system without migration costs) shows an annual operating cost savings of 42%. Power consumption alone is reduced by 84%.

Hardware and system software costs, including service/support, are reduced by 67%.

Table 2-1: Budget Example: Packaged Food Company
(in 1,000s of dollars)

	1992	1993	1994	1995
HP System (Starting Third Quarter, 1992)				
HW/SW/Networking	52	105	105	105
Training/Consultants	45	0	0	0
HW/SW/Support	9	35	35	35
Power	2	6	6	6
Subtotal	108	146	146	146
Proprietary Mainframe				
Service	82	41	0	0
Lease	126	53	0	0
Power	44	22	0	0
Subtotal	252	116	0	0
Migration Services	59	117	117	117
Total Budget	418	378	263	263
Budget without Migration Costs	359	261	146	146
Steady-State Operating Cost Comparison				
Proprietary Mainframe	252			
HP System	146	(58% of mainframe costs)		

The downsizing figures in Table 2-1 are conservative because they do not take into account potential MIS staff savings. The MIS director is harboring plans to use the money saved through downsizing to launch a subsequent program for adding new UNIX and client/server functionality, and will need staff to accomplish this. The end result is likely to be a more costly system, but one packed with much more capability.

Savings from downsizing MIS staff can be quite substantial. Managers at NI Industries claim that staff savings were the most significant area in their downsizing program (from an IBM 3083 to an

HP server), reducing their 1991 budget by $475,000. They had considered themselves a fairly lean IBM shop with 12 people, but today the new environment allows them to get by with 6. They also claim that software on the HP platform costs less, about 50% less than equivalent software on the prior IBM machine, and maintenance is down 65%. "The cost reduction is just astounding!" exclaimed Kristel Lacy, MIS director at Norris, a division of NI Industries, during an interview in late 1992.

Holstein Association

Another user organization willing to share the details of its downsizing budget is Holstein Association, the global records keeper for Holstein cow lineage. Holstein is a non-profit membership organization of over 50,000 members and is the largest dairy breed organization in the world. Holstein keeps data on over 12 million Holstein cows on its active and historical data bases. All purebred registered Holsteins can be traced back to 8,800 animals imported from Holland in the nineteenth century. Purebred Holstein cows for which lineage can be clearly traced to the original imported herd are recorded in the Holstein "Herd Book" database. They fetch a higher price on the market for frozen embryos (as much as $20,000 per embryo) and sperm, and sell for a premium as well. Other cows with traceable Holstein lineage of three generations are accommodated in an "Identified Holstein Friesian" database, providing them status second only to the Herd Book cows in terms of pedigree.

Individual cows are checked annually by "classification scorers" from the Holstein Association to assess traits directly related to the economic value of the cow, i.e., birthing ease, susceptibility to disease, etc. According to Holstein Association, "These scored traits are genetically transmittable to a statistically predictable extent as well, so the degree to which they are present has direct bearing on the dollar value of the animal's (and the animal's parent's) saleable stored "genetic products," i.e., sperm or frozen embryos. Classification scorer information is input nightly and cross-referenced in the database files with other related information, such as the quality and amount of each cow's milk.

Information in the database is used for a variety of purposes. Sometimes Holstein breed improvement programs are operated across national boundaries using the data to improve milk production of a foreign herd. Recently, sperm from Holstein "Super Cows" (cows exceeding in economic manageability i.e., high disease resistance, lower food consumption, high birthing success rate, and excellent milk production (35,000 to 50,000 pounds of milk per year) was used to create similar offspring in Eastern block countries, where the average milk output is a meager 10,000 pounds of milk per year. But for the most part, the database is used to produce reports for agribusiness farmers, to help them better understand the transmission of traits to progeny and to prove pedigree for the trade of cow sperm and embryos. Reports usually take from two to three days to produce.

The main set of Holstein records resides on an IDMS mainframe database, and the purebred pedigree Herd Book information resides on a mainframe VSAM. Rick Burque, Holstein's New Technology Analyst, has wanted for a long time to help improve Holstein's service to the larger agribusiness users by providing them with custom printouts better addressing their individual needs, and perhaps even direct access to the database itself. A few years back, Holstein MIS management was sold on the data accessibility benefits of IDMS over VSAM and went through the painstaking process of learning a new language and porting most of the database over to IDMS (the Herd Book remained on VSAM). Even though IDMS was clearly superior to VSAM, Holstein MIS soon wondered whether they had been too optimistic. After the IDMS porting program had been completed, their initial practice runs showed that providing the numerous Holstein Association users ad hoc query access to the IDMS network-model database system would quickly exceed capacity and bring the system down.

The MIS team then moved ahead with a program to reduce input workload, starting with data input activities. They introduced handheld DAP Technology units for classification scorers to use in the field. Substantial ruggedness is required for these handheld terminals because classifiers work outdoors year round in conditions ranging from the dust and heat of California deserts to the subzero cold of Wisconsin winters. Many of the classifiers have to literally chase cows through the fields to accomplish their missions. The DAP units Holstein chose were developed for use by the logging and mining industries in Canada. They even pass water immersion tests, according to Mr. Burque. At the end of the day, the classification scorers simply plug in a modem and upload their reports to the mainframe database for processing.

The program is working fine, but the MIS staff still find themselves with a mounting workload. They are stuck at the office on weekends a month at a time two times a year, producing a "Sire Summary" book, which requires an update to the various databases for over 1.5 million cows, does an exhaustive statistical cross-comparison of genetic traits, and establishes a revised ranking of the top 100 and top 400 U.S. registered Holstein bulls based on the new statistical information. One ongoing frustration with the mainframe system has been the length of time it takes to carry out a single COBOL compile, typically 10-20 minutes.

The MIS team was faced with a decision to either upgrade to an ES9000 or move to an alternative technology. As they started their inquiry, the database accessibility afforded by INFORMIX relational databases caught their attention. Further investigation showed that INFORMIX could provide the type of data reports Holstein was looking for, and UNIX servers from HP could power the system at a much lower cost. Holstein MIS management looked at the 500,000 to 800,000 lines of code they would need to rewrite (much of it to be rewritten again from IDMS) and built up the courage to convince their team to learn yet another language, and move to a very different world of computing. Mr. Burque maintains that the main reason for MIS management's decision to move was not cost savings, but rather to gain better access to data for their customers. Even during the initial stages of the transition, they expect to start providing on-demand pedigree services by fax.

Holstein MIS's investigation turned up effective methods for linking the new INFORMIX database to IDMS. The utility they chose was Express from Horizon Technologies of Needham, Massachusetts, which provides LU6.2 IBM protocol-based information transfer in both IDMS and UNIX environments. They put together a plan for moving to the new system and redesigning the data for easier tagging, sorting, and searching. The MIS team believes the rewriting will all have to be done meticulously by hand, but the end-product should be well worth the effort. Their projected budget appears in Table 2-2, and shows savings of close to 4 to 1 in the later years. Figures in this table reflect Holstein's best-guess estimates based on data available prior to final contract negotiations. Additionally, expense projections beyond 1993 are based on currently available equipment, prices, and technology.

As mentioned above, Holstein MIS management plans to restructure all databases and recode the inventory of database applications individually over a four-year period, converting each from a network to a relational database model, and thus will need to keep the IBM 4381 running during that period. MIS departments at other companies operating databases with more easily transferable structures can usually cut over and realize downsizing benefits sooner,

**Table 2-2: Holstein Downsizing Budget Projection
(in 1,000s of dollars)**

	1992	1993	1994	1995	1996	1997	1998	1999
New System (HP 847/827 Servers)								
HW Lease:	11	100	173	210	220	140	67	15
SW License:	28	220	108	31	2	2	2	2
Support:	11	107	113	114	116	121	121	121
Training:	40	29	24	12	12	12	12	12
Consulting:	25	12	11	10	0	0	0	0
Total New System Costs:	115	468	429	377	350	275	202	150
Concurrent Mainframe Costs (IBM 4381)	365	383	402	423	222	0	0	0
Total Budget During Migration:	480	851	831	800	572	275	202	150
Total Budget If Upgraded To ES9000:	365	598	620	643	667	585	559	559
Migration vs. Upgrade:	+115	+253	+211	+157	-95	-310	-357	-409

with the help of the translation tools available today. The packaged foods company from the previous example was able to choose a faster route.

Holstein MIS management took their projections to the Holstein board which is made up of the most influential farmers in the Holstein industry and gave a compelling pitch for extra money to undertake this challenging migration. Squeezing out funds for aggressive programs is difficult at most non-profit organizations, and The Holstein Association is no exception. The MIS pitch was a clear and articulate summary of their views. I have included it verbatim for reference by future downsizers:

Even though the cost of downsizing is significantly less expensive in the long run, as shown in the attached financial analysis, there are more important reasons to downsize. Workstations will allow us to develop new programs and systems faster. The handheld computer was programmed on a PC and was completed in about a third of the time of what it would have taken on the mainframe. The new system will be more powerful. We now run the same programs in 4 days on the workstation that took 28 days on the mainframe. And finally, the new system will allow us to organize the data better in order to produce reports and products faster.

He also included a list of downsizing benefits in his presentation:

- Reduced cost of computing for hardware and software; Lots more processing power and capabilities for your dollar.
- More powerful programming tools and languages to increase programmer productivity and reduce development and maintenance time.
- Improved database technology which will allow us to better structure our data in order to provide information in the format we need and at the time we need it.
- Hardware equipment is much smaller in size; 1700 square feet of computer room space freed for potential rental property in year 1997; using a current rental charge of $12-$14 per square foot per year would net a potential annual income of $23,800-$20,400.
- Significantly lower power requirements to operate equipment and no special air conditioning requirements; approximately $20,000 in savings per year for electrical power beginning in year 1995.
- Increased flexibility to add, change, or remove hardware and software components as needed; ability to add incremental processing power.
- Increased flexibility by having many options available for future hardware and software decisions; downsizing will allow us to take advantage of (1) a mix of products from a variety of vendors and (2) the cut throat competition in the industry. We will not be tied to a single vendor with a proprietary environment as we currently are with our IBM mainframe.
- User friendly graphic screens are available to improve user productivity (through windowing technology).
- All computing resources can be connected together—eliminate the "islands of information."
- Proven technology with many success stories; other companies have successfully downsized and unplugged their mainframes.

The board responded favorably and voted to fund the proposal.

During an interview in late 1992, Mr. Burque contrasted the HP downsizing program accepted by Holstein with an alternate approach that had been originally considered by Holstein MIS based on the IBM AS/400 technical platform: "The lack of an available industry-standard GUI such as OSF/Motif, as well as the absence of widely-used third-party database engines, such as INFORMIX, on the AS/400 would have severely limited the sophistication and portability of the applications we would be creating. Faced with the prospect of spending millions to deliver a suite of out-of-date menu-driven information systems dependent on the idiosyncracies of one vendor's proprietary technology, we decided that this was not something we could endorse to the board as being in Holstein's best long-term interest."

Now with the budget in hand, Holstein MIS is managing the implementation program issues. The MIS management team has brought their staff of 20 programmers through many transitions, VSAM to IDMS, IDMS to PCs, now to INFORMIX and UNIX. The current change is seen as more drastic than before, but MIS managers are hoping their planned training sessions will be sufficient to get their staff up to speed. They also hope the MIS team members will be motivated to learn INFORMIX 4GL and realize that INFORMIX skills can be as important (if not more important) on their future résumés as years of COBOL programming in the IBM mainframe environment. Mr. Burque commented that hc hopes they will notice the high-paying INFORMIX jobs advertised in today's trade journals.

With the new capabilities Holstein MIS is already discovering on their new system, they have little reason to look back. Mr. Burque comments, "In the Holstein DOS/VSE IDMS environment, procedures were difficult to store in the database, and debugging with IDMS was also a bear...with INFORMIX we can do all of this and more. These are the capabilities we should have had from the beginning."

Downsizing to Upsize the Business: IT-Preneuring

If we talk again in a year with the packaged food company high-lighted in Chapter 2, we are likely to hear a different story. The MIS director will probably be in the throes of implementing client/server, re-engineering the business, and coincidentally increasing MIS cost. We can expect his comments at that time to focus on business value, and we may get a yawn if we ask about cost reduction. Some of the other companies we interviewed for this book were either far enough along in their programs to have already reached this stage, or had focused on business value generation from the start. MIS managers at these companies easily fit the category of IT-preneur mentioned in the Preface. They are information technology managers looking to expand their company's business by harnessing the power of newer distributed computing technologies.

As I opened my interview with Liteline Clothing's Bill Williams (pseudonyms) with a summary of some of the cost savings other companies had reported, he stopped me and asked me a question on this very subject.

MIS as a Business Generator

Liteline Clothing

"Do you want to know why we are downsizing to a distributed topology?" asked Mr. Williams, the MIS director of Liteline Clothing, a major producer and distributor of cotton and polyester lightweight garments. The MIS operations budget today is less than $3.5 million. That is 1.5% of gross sales for Liteline. Even if I drove MIS costs to zero, that would only save Liteline $3.5 million. By contrast, if I provide the appropriate information to the right people and increase Liteline's revenues...that is a totally different story. The upside revenue potential is much greater than the opportunity for cost reduction! The cost savings are there but that is not the reason to go to distributed platforms."

Bill Williams and his team are in the process of reducing operational costs to below $1.75 million over the next three years by moving to HP UNIX servers. The road they took to get there has been anything but straight. A leveraged buy-out (LBO), and the separation of two former Liteline businesses, Liteline and Warmline Clothing (also a pseudonym) was the start of the journey. Before the LBO, both organizations relied on two IBM 3083J mainframes to do information processing. After the businesses were separated, the Warmline managers downsized their operations to a network of AS/400s, and Liteline Clothing was left running the 3083J mainframe at only 70% capacity.

Liteline management has a strong belief that MIS should be an important partner in generating business. New challenges presented by aggressive competitors and changes in the structure of the business, have raised the bar for Liteline many times in the past. MIS has often been an integral force for taking the bar and raising it to new heights. An important turning point in business awareness at MIS occurred in 1978 with the acquisition of Rainbowgear (a pseudonym), a producer of women's sports apparel. With that acquisition, Liteline was suddenly thrown into the dynamic and challenging world of fashion goods.

Rainbowgear brought in a vast line of products with hundreds of color variations. The acquisition of this new fashion business meant a complete reworking of the information systems to not only handle the sudden explosion of product line items, but also to speed up the development cycle for new products. Without a responsive information systems infrastructure, Liteline simply could not keep up.

Mr. Williams has seen MIS's business challenges increase steadily after that date as well. "Before, it was enough to keep on top of inventory turns and ensure top quality in the products delivered. Today, high quality and efficient inventory control are givens. The only real area of differentiation is customer service." What Mr. Williams means by customer service goes far beyond superb sales and support to the major retailers selling Liteline products. He believes one way Liteline has gained an edge in this highly competitive market is by using retail information to provide superior "replenishment" advice on how to effectively stock retail shelves with Liteline products. Liteline representatives work with MIS to analyze point of sale (POS) data supplied by retail chains on Liteline's products (the retailers keep information on competing brands confidential). They then use the information to advise customers on how to adjust product mix and shelf space by season, geography, and even store location for achieving maximum inventory turns. Increased sales of Liteline products translates into higher revenues for both companies.

This type of replenishment strategy has become a high priority for both U.S. retailers and their suppliers. Replenishment has a demonstrated track record for improving shelf space utilization and generating revenue. The Liteline MIS team members know of surveys showing that customers "who can't find what they are looking for at one store will complete their purchase 80% of the time somewhere else." Getting the right merchandise on the store shelf at the right time for the right people is the name of the game...a game that is impossible to play today without timely and detailed product turnover information at the POS.

Mr. Williams and his team have felt for many years that IBM was the appropriate choice for Liteline. In his words, "MIS at Liteline was all blue (completely IBM) until 1988 because we thought IBM was the low-cost supplier...not in terms of product cost, but in terms of getting the job done. We feel that system downtime was more expensive than anything else in our business, and so even though IBM equipment and services cost more, IBM's all-encompassing support capabilities with only one number to call for any problem made them the winners." Liteline is a premier user of IBM's Netview networking management system. The Liteline team has pushed the technology to the limit. They have used Netview and other tools to automate most things in the shop, and through automation, the operations staff was reduced from 52 people in 1986 to 25 in 1991.

As mentioned above, after the LBO, Liteline Clothing was left with excess capacity, which translated into a very high fixed cost percentage in the MIS operations budget. Not only did the MIS team want to eliminate the wasted mainframe capacity, but they also wanted to use this change in systems as an opportunity to enhance MIS business effectiveness. With the IBM system, it was difficult to carry out replenishment analysis with sufficient granularity. The information really had to be by product and store. A large department store, for instance, in a high-income neighborhood with more elderly clientele needs to stock a completely different set of items than another outlet of the same chain in a less well-off neighborhood. Seasonal adjustments in products and styles raise time pressure by making last month's information obsolete. In this type of interactive world, mainframe and hierarchical database information bottlenecks cannot be tolerated.

With this in mind, the team took a hard look at the IMS database, which had given them only one reliability problem during 17 years of active service tracking Liteline's products, and realized that the IMS architecture could not take them any further. Mr. Williams comments, "IMS is extremely good at what it does. Perhaps the limited accessibility inherent in the IMS design has been partially responsible for the integrity and security we have enjoyed with IMS all these years...but unfortunately the rule of life with IMS is navigation...you have to be a skilled programmer to get the information you want."

As Mr. Williams set out to explore alternatives, he had in the back of his mind a vision for better aligning his MIS team's capabilities with the requirements of Liteline's business managers. Instead of leading a team of technical gurus, he wanted to change the skill mix of his team to 80% business analyst and 20% technical. He believed that computers had evolved sufficiently to allow for this type of change. Mr. Williams described what he refers to as a classic example of the old mentality of computing, "I went to a party and was told by a proud mother that she is sending her son Johnny to computer science class to learn computers...I asked her whether she sewed clothing and she replied she did...and then I asked her whether she knew how a sewing machine worked. She admitted that she didn't. My point was that you do not necessarily need to know the innards of a computer to use it effectively." Mr. Williams wants his team to worry less about the way computers work and more about what to do with them.

He started his investigation by asking two vendors he and the other management members knew well, IBM and DEC, to propose new IS solutions. The proposals were to also include appropriate CASE tools and relational database technologies for shielding his staff from having to know system idiosyncrasies. During the inquiry, MIS managers also heard that HP might be able to provide an affordable solution, and so a proposal was received from HP as well. Initial system cost and five year internal rates of return (IRR) on the proposals were compared, and HP came out ahead on both counts: 1/3 better on system price and 26% higher on IRR.

The MIS team then focused on ensuring proof of concept...with special interest on testing whether the HP solution would be commercially robust and otherwise capable of meeting their needs. The first step was to find appropriate CASE tools for the HP system, i.e., tools that cover the complete development cycle, are seamless to the developer, never discard any data or development history, document everything, and are not dependent on any hardware platform. The CASE tool suite they found from Texas Instruments, called IEF (Integrated Engineering Facility), surpassed the alternative they were considering with the DEC proposal. The TI IEF tool fits the bill so well in fact that Mr. Williams does not expect to train many of his staff in C language (the basic development language for the UNIX environment). He finds that TI's IEF generates 100% of the C code error-free. He now hopes that, with the exception of a few C language experts to develop and maintain bridging software to the IBM AS/400s and System 370s, most of his staff members will not pick up much C language. "Any work done directly in C," comments Mr. Williams, "would, by definition, not be done with the CASE tools, not documented in TI IEF, and not easy to support."

The MIS team also checked out relational databases and open system network management tools for the HP system. They had heard that security, integrity, and system management were potential areas of weakness with UNIX, but the shortcomings they found appeared surmountable. The team also felt comfortable with their assessment of the network management capabilities of SNMP (Simple Network Management Protocol) and HP's OpenView tools. Mr. Williams remarked, "A lot of what we need is there, if not on day one, very soon in the future."

Liteline Clothing decided on the HP solution and put in place a plan to port the customer, product, and personnel data from IMS to an Oracle relational database over the next 2-3 years. The MIS team was satisfied with their selection of CASE tools and databases, but no matter how hard they searched, they could not find an appropriate application package to meet Liteline's special pricing requirements. Liteline needs to frequently change pricing by promotion, rather than product line, and few application packages provide this feature. The MIS team is constructing a custom application for this function using the IEF tools. For the most part, however, they plan to use new off-the-shelf applications for fulfilling standard company functions, such as accounting, finance, and personnel.

After making the decision to move to open systems, the MIS team immediately outsourced Liteline's mainframe operations. This allowed Liteline to treat the MF capacity as a variable cost during the transition. The MIS team has dismantled the existing mainframe system, and is busy with what they feel is an extremely valuable transition program. "I have never had the opportunity to work on a project for which the business case shows such an incredibly high internal rate of return!" exclaims Mr. Williams.

Bill Williams and his team were able to demonstrate the more tangible MIS cost reduction advantages as well as the less concrete business benefits to gain board approval for his program, but what about programs for which the cost of adding strategic functionality exceed the reductions in mainframe costs? How can an MIS director sell a client/server program for which the costs may actually go up?

American Airlines found as their MIS department began implementing an enterprise-wide "neural network" for increased functionality, that the new system would not decrease computing charges to end-user departments. It in fact noticeably increased their costs. MIS managers therefore needed not only to make the business case for top management, but also to each impacted end user community as well. A business case had to be put together for each department of the global airline!

This was not an environment for rapid-fire roll out of the entire network, as Wayne Pendleton was quick to find out during the initial implementation phase. The American Airlines story is a study not only of changing technology but also of social change in large business organizations...and moreover, of how it does not take an MBA to do a business case.

Pushing the Frontiers of Management Science with Information Systems

American Airlines

Using information systems for strategic advantage is old hat at American, the $13 billion air transportation industry giant. Client/server in the hands of this information technology master is likely to go beyond strategy in the normal sense and bring about major changes in American's work practices and organizational structure over the next five years, predicted a 1990 *Harvard Business Review* article authored by Max Hopper, American's Vice

President of Information Systems.[1] By 1992, progress had been made, but the organizational and cultural obstacles encountered have been significant. Wayne Pendleton, American's Managing Director of Advanced Office Systems, is building the information infrastructure to realize the vision expressed by Mr. Hopper, even in the face of dwindling industry profits.

American Airlines is recognized as a leader in generating business value from mainframe-based information technology. American's well-known SABRE reservation system, developed in the 1960s for airline reservation agents, still dominates the world of Computer Reservation Systems (CRS). Already in the mid-1970s, the SABRE system was much more than a reservation system. Its features included such functions as flight planning, tracking spare parts, scheduling crews, and developing a range of decision support systems for management. After 1976, SABRE became a common fixture on the desks of travel agents and included a full set of capabilities for hotel, rail, rental car reservations, etc. The same *Harvard Business Review* article illustrates SABRE's profound impact on the airline industry with data on the increase in tickets purchased through travel agents. Travel agent ticket sales rose from 40% of all ticket sales in 1976, to become the dominant channel in 1990 with 80% of tickets issued.

SABRE's early origin, of course, places it well before the era of client/server technology. American Airlines had jointly worked with IBM to develop the proprietary SABRE operating system (now called TPF) and the 6-bit networking system that it still operates on today. As with many of the first successful applications developed, SABRE's uniqueness makes it incompatible with other systems. This incompatibility has, in turn, led to a proliferation of hardware terminal monitors on the desks of American Airlines' knowledge workers. In addition to needing a desktop SABRE terminal, each worker also requires a dumb terminal to access MVS management and accounting programs residing on mainframes. Moreover, many also use a PC for summarizing, analyzing, and repackaging the data from the two other systems...much of which they enter by hand while viewing the other screens.

Rather than simply putting together a program of one-for-three swaps (a desktop PC for three terminals), American Airlines, in true Max Hopper fashion, took on a much loftier mission, that of building

1. Hopper, Max D. "Rattling SABRE—New Ways to Compete on Information," *Harvard Business Review*, May–Jun. 1990, 118–125.

an enterprise-wide technology platform that is, in Max Hopper's words, "an organizational resource that individuals and groups can use to build new systems and procedures to do their jobs smarter, better, and more creatively." To achieve this vision, American Airlines embarked on developing an "electronic nervous system" that would:

- Give each employee access to the entire system through a single, easy-to-use workstation
- Connect all managerial levels and computing centers within the company
- Generate hard-dollar savings quantifiable in advance
- Be as much an organizational redesign effort as a technology implementation program, to ensure the work processes take best advantage of the IT investments

The system is dubbed "InterAAct," with the American Airlines logo in the middle. Mr. Pendleton sees the ultimate goal of the program as pushing decision-making down far into American Airlines' organization, and thereby lowering organization cost and increasing flexibility for better responding to American's rapidly changing environment.

This project did not come out of the blue. Like many other companies, American's user community was becoming increasingly frustrated. MIS had been backlogged with requests to add features to the system and could not be responsive enough to keep users from looking for what appeared to be better ways to resolve their problems. Although American had standardized on many in-house technologies, isolated user groups brought in system integration consultants and created what Mr. Pendleton refers to as non-standard system "mushrooms," sometimes with disastrous results. Users with mushroom projects found themselves taking on more work than they had bargained for. Non-compliant systems brought on extra duties, such as back-up, recoveries, etc., that MIS could not be responsible for. Soon these users found themselves coming back to MIS to ask for relief from the support burden and MIS members found themselves reworking the systems to comply with enterprise standards to make them feasible for central system management.

The user cause, however, was not ignored; it was, in fact, championed from the very top of the company. Bob Crandall, Chairman of American Airlines, reviewed proposals from several vendors and concluded that they only gave lip service to end user requirements. He then assigned a group of representative knowledge workers to develop the most appropriate system for achieving the new networked office automation vision. These empowered users worked closely with MIS to determine system feature and design requirements, and to select appropriate hardware and software partners.

The highly motivated user group developed a detailed request for proposal (RFP) describing the environment they envisioned...one with exceptional ease-of-use, access to the whole corporate environment from each workstation, and unlimited availability to corporate data (within security constraints). Cost, although important, came secondary in their minds. Of the three competing vendors (IBM, DEC, and HP), HP was chosen because HP's proposal came closest to fulfilling all the RFP requirements.

Mr. Pendleton's department did not plan to waste time deploying the new server and PC LAN infrastructure. He aimed at installing 13,000 (!) nodes over the first two years. His department of 110 IS members provided system installation and an optional one-day training course for end users on the new graphical user interface environment and the electronic mail function. Then his plans went slightly awry. It is now four years later and he has yet to install his 6,000th node.

The program has not stopped by any means...initial user resistance led Mr. Pendleton to decide on a six-month hiatus, after which he has continued rolling out the program at a slower pace—the pace at which end users feel comfortable introducing the new technology to their work environment and taking on the new user responsibilities inherent in a distributed computing system. Tougher economic conditions have also led to the reigning-in of IS expenses, slowing the pace of the program roll-out even more.

Much of the resistance focused on work place and billing changes brought on with the new systems. End-user department managers were now required, in addition to taking care of some expanded systems activities at their location, to also foot the bill for their department systems. These same entities had paid information systems charges through allocated overhead in the past, but those charges had appeared to be more broadly distributed. The end-user department managers also soon found that the single-screen GUI desktop PCs being installed for the new network cost more (although just slightly more) than the three boxes previously populating their desks.

Mr. Pendleton realized the miscalculation and quickly changed the mission of his department from "technology provision" to "joint information technology partnering with department users." This change of mission transformed Mr. Pendleton's staff into internal "tech marketers," working closely with business management teams to help them understand the impact of the new infrastructure on their departments, estimate new system costs, adjust the system offering to better meet their individual business needs, and develop business cases for each organization.

As Mr. Pendleton became more flexible with the system offering, he became more stringent about user responsibilities. The training courses which had previously been optional, now became mandatory to ensure that users gained a basic working knowledge of the system. Mr. Pendleton also required divisions to assign "IT facilitators" to take on non-technical system work, such as first-level IS support and scheduling for training, and to provide continuity in the ongoing technology improvement efforts.

The business cases jointly developed by Mr. Pendleton's MIS staff and American's end users demonstrate the potency of process re-engineering enabled by the new enterprise network infrastructure. One regional office of 700 marketing representatives, for instance, is proposing a quick payback on the introduction of rep notebook PCs linked to the network by modem. The portable PCs may allow the office managers to take the heroic step of completely eliminating their office building and desks, thereby generating savings far exceeding the cost of the new systems. The reps would then work out of their homes and meet in conference rooms when they need to get together.

American's European and Pacific organizations were able to justify installation of international electronic mail through a reduction in telephone line usage; more mail means less chatting over expensive voice lines. Others have justified the costs through anticipated future revenues, but "that is often more difficult to track," according to Mr. Pendleton.

Mr. Pendleton sees their current status as "still building the highway." The major system changes inherent in the first phase rollout are:

- Standardizing the user interface on an easy-to-use NewWave GUI with object-oriented capabilities (the object-oriented capabilities are to be fully leveraged with future system enhancements)
- Installation of HP's electronic HPDESK mail system, to allow for easy communication among American's 110,000 employees

- Standardizing network components by changing:
  - Token Ring LANs to Ethernet
  - IPX protocol to TCP/IP
  - 6-bit SABRE leased line to X.25 packet switching

NOTE: Differences in protocol had forced American Airlines to depend on problematic gateways between Ethernet and Token Ring LANs, as well as to develop bilingual PCs fluent in both IPX and TCP/IP. The final protocol decisions were made less based on component functionality and more on the potential for interoperability with all American Airline platforms.

Mr. Hopper envisions a world of full-fledged decentralized electronic decision making at American Airlines. In his words, "The role of management will change from overseeing and control, to resolving important problems and transferring best practices throughout the organization." But this world is still many IS implementation programs away. Few of the decision support applications and business processes for bringing this world to life are in place yet, and most of the current applications still reside on the mainframe.

Mr. Pendleton comments, "What we are implementing now is similar to the initial U.S. government highway projects of the 1960s. Once the highways were completed, there was a tremendously beneficial impact on many parts of the U.S. economy. Towns blossomed into cities and new businesses emerged along the new traffic arteries to cater to the increasingly mobile U.S. population. It would have been crazy to build the hotels and restaurants before the highway was put in place." Both Mr. Pendleton and Mr. Hopper are anxiously awaiting the day their electronic highway transforms the landscape of American Airlines...and so is the Society for Information Management. This well-known organization awarded American Airlines the 1991 "Partners in Leadership Award" for developing InterAAct, and pushing the frontiers of applying information technology for business success.

Why Is Everyone Taking so Long?

Given the compelling strategic reasons for client/server and the demonstrated bottom line impact of downsizing, why are people taking so long to move over? From the looks of it, most mainframe shops in the U.S. could achieve substantial benefits (even in the near term) by making the move. Yet, many companies are still stuck at the investigation phase. This question may have already been partially answered by the downsizing experiences illustrated in prior chapters. Downsizing is not simple, and moving to client/server topologies is even more complex. Moreover, the risk of starting a major IS project and having it turn into a runaway drain on the financial and management resources of a company can be quite high, even if the technologies are better known.

According to articles in the press, it has taken Marriott, the highly successful U.S. hotel and restaurant chain, eight years of working with UNIX in different Marriott organizations, and the frustrating experience of being entangled in a system development fiasco (not of their own doing) using more traditional technologies, before setting sights on an open system downsizing solution for a major portion of its mission-critical central reservations system. Open systems technology has also come a long way during that time, making the transition more feasible.

Few companies can fit their systems and IS requirements into a generic downsizing template. Every company (both MIS and management members included) has its own, sometimes winding, path to forge.

This chapter compares the paths of two highly successful medium-sized companies making the move from outdated platforms to open systems. These two companies, both on a short fuse toward shooting their mainframes, have achieved excellent business success thanks to highly effective and entrepreneurial founding management teams. Their successes, however, have been achieved in spite of, rather than due to, their information systems. Both have made similar decisions to downsize, but the way each is going about it, contrasts significantly. This chapter also offers suggestions on how companies embarking on a path today can cut through their own particular set of brambles and more quickly arrive at an appropriate downsizing solution.

Are Your Information Systems Really Making a Difference?

Delight, Inc. and Mediply

What does a leading producer and distributor of cakes, pastry, and other desserts have in common with a major distributor of medical materials and equipment? Both have found clear keys for success in their market niches and both could NOT leverage their potential information system strengths to get where they are today.

Delight (a pseudonym) was the first to provide desserts on a nationwide scale that could truly be passed off as "homemade." Superior ingredients, recipes, and company-owned refrigerated transport placed semi-finished Delight products in the hands of proud homemakers around the country. All that was necessary to serve the last sweet course of a family feast, was some quick finishing touches (thawing, microwaving, or baking). As Delight's desserts became as "American as Apple Pie," Delight's volumes became sufficient to maintain rock bottom prices (Delight's cakes today go for only $2.00 to $3.00 in the local supermarket), and few distributors have been willing to risk expensive refrigerated shelf space to try another "homemade" brand. Major supermarket chains throughout the U.S. have provided little opportunity for competitors to share Delight's coveted refrigerated racks.

Delight's hold on the refrigerated display is almost as strong as Mediply's (another pseudonym) grip on smaller medical clinics around the country. Mediply realized early on that physicians did not want to be bothered with ordering materials and equipment from multiple suppliers. After all, most physicians do not feel they went through grueling years at medical school to learn how to order materials, and many medical offices are not large enough to hire a dedicated medical supplies purchasing agent. Mediply management focused on expanding product line breadth to ensure their customers had no need to go anywhere else for supplies. Their offerings stretch from daily consumables (cotton swabs, gauze, paper and cloth outfits, gargle, etc.) to more durable medical clinic equipment (patient chairs, diagnostic instruments, illumination devices, etc.). Currently they have over 30,000 items on their price list, more than the number of items at many clothing retailers. Mediply expanded its presence and dominated this market niche by helping physicians protect the most important asset in their office, their own time. Mediply's all-encompassing line of supplies, moreover, helped lock in the customer. Few openings were left by their span of offerings for narrow-line competitors to break through. Smaller competitors soon found that undercutting Mediply's price on say, gargle or patient chairs, was not enough to gain a foothold. They immediately hit up against the harsh reality that underlies Mediply's success. A simple discount on a few supplies is not attractive enough to convince the busy physician to spend his valuable time checking out a new line of products, and, on an ongoing basis, fill out a separate order in addition to Mediply's just to save a few pennies.

Both Delight and Mediply know how to provide a special value and lock in their customers. But talk with the MIS directors at these companies and you will hear that the companies have achieved their success in spite of, rather than because of, their information systems.

The world of information systems, however, has changed for these companies during the past two years. Both have new MIS directors, and both are now sufficiently fed up with their mainframe-based systems to decide to jettison their "Old Iron" over the next six months.

For Mediply, a change in top management was the turning point in the decision to downsize. Immediately after Mediply was acquired a year ago, the new owners brought in a systems integration company, SIC (a pseudonym). SIC's mission was to migrate from the current 4381 series IBM mainframe and IBM system 36 configuration, to a more distributed architecture based on IBM AS/400 midrange servers.

In a September 1992 interview, Mike Mickel (also a pseudonym), the SIC manager now in charge of many of Mediply's MIS activities, described the MIS bottleneck he found at Mediply when he appeared on the scene in 1991. According to Mr. Mickel, Mediply's managers had given up on using the computer system for many of the critical business tasks either because important functionality had not been included in the patchwork of development fixes applied to the 15-year-old order entry and inventory systems, or because the response time was too slow to support productive work. Regional terminals connected to system 36s in the distribution centers sometimes took as long as 15 seconds to respond to a simple instruction. Winning in Mediply's business requires close management attention to important distribution costs and margins, but the system was not designed to monitor pricing by product category, and inventory levels had become such a mystery that physical inspection of the warehouses was carried out on a periodic basis just to check the numbers. The type of computer reporting of revenues and gross margin by region, supplier, or account enjoyed by most companies, was still just an aspiration to the Mediply management team. The MIS department struggled in a reactive mode to fix "system problems" from an ever-increasing list of backlog requests. The management team had long ago given up trying to get the information systems to work for them, and had hired staff to calculate the most important reports by hand.

Even with all their business savvy, the prior Mediply management team had only a limited understanding of computers. Mediply MIS employees tell stories of a top executive who mistook a microfiche machine for a PC. To the management team's credit, they tried several times to find a new information systems vendor who could help solve their system problems. But the vendor proposals either appeared too radical or promised fewer improvements than they felt were necessary, so they were left in an indefinite holding pattern at "status quo." It is unlikely that Mediply would be shooting the mainframe today without the strong influence of the new owners.

The move at Delight, by contrast, was the result of a natural changing of the guard in the MIS department. The prior MIS director retired and the new MIS director, Ian Inman (a pseudonym) left his MIS position at a major package foods company to take his place, bringing a new level of MIS expertise with him.

Shortly after Mr. Inman's arrival at Delight, he found to his dismay that an upgraded version of the aging mainframe had been ordered and was soon to be delivered from overseas. He immediately tried to negotiate a cancellation of the delivery, but things had gone too far to back out without significant cancellation penalties. Mr. Inman let us know why he was so anxious to return the mainframe. He explained that his problems stem from the mainframe vendor's proprietary nature, and the vendor's small and shrinking 5% U.S. market share. Mr. Inman saw few, if any, application SW packages or utilities for the vendor's platforms forthcoming from independent software houses. Most applications would need to be developed in-house. Moreover, the vendor did not appear to have the resources to staff service centers close enough to their customers. Delight was left with an 800 long-distance service and support number to call. The closest potential back-up site in case of a system crash was another customer 50 miles away. Mr. Inman jokingly points out that the vendor must have expected them to be protected by "The grace of God." MIS managers at Delight had become accustomed to the vendor's information system/support lethargy in much the same way that Mediply managers had put up with 15-second response time on their systems. When their mainframe vendor reported that it could take a week to ship replacement disks for some that had unexpectedly failed, few were surprised.

Mr. Inman knew about the cost, functionality, and flexibility advantages of open systems from press articles and attending executive seminars at Cambridge Technology Group, a well-known Massachusetts firm providing executive education and open systems integration services. Since HP had been featured as a leading vendor in many of the articles Mr. Inman had read, he included HP in his search for a vendor to replace the mainframe. After inspecting the HP offering and checking references, he also found sufficient commercial robustness and cost reduction potential in HP systems to decide to make his move. "The three year difference in service costs alone came to $150,000. These cost savings are to be realized even with expanded service hours and substantially enhanced system capacity. We are adding two DAT (Digital Audio Tape) storage units, expanding memory from 30 to 290 gigabytes, and increasing disk space from 12 to 24 gigabytes. The service hours will increase from 9X5 (9 hours, 5 days a week) to round-the-clock 24x7 support," Mr. Inman commented during a telephone interview in early 1993.

Mr. Inman's estimates for reduction in overall system operating costs are just as dramatic—they are to drop by a precipitous 42%.

The mainframe vendor's managers put some extra nails in their own coffin after the news got to them about Delight's rejection of their upgrade system. Delight's MIS staff members were shocked to hear for the first time from the vendor's pleading sales reps that they had been marketing UNIX systems for the prior two years and had never let Delight know. So much for what was left of that vendor's proprietary margins.

Although both of these companies were clearly dissatisfied with their systems, and both have decided to rapidly unwind their mainframes, their motivations were slightly different. Mediply's applications and platform are clearly inadequate for supporting their 12,000-product-line business. Delight's packaged foods business is inherently less complex, and so the application software shortcomings are less distressing than the underlying systems software and hardware platform inconveniences. This difference in motivations has, in turn, led to different migration paths for the two companies. Mediply is replacing the bulk of its mainframe applications with new open systems application packages from an independent systems integrator. Delight is moving the mainframe code over "as-is" to the new open systems platform using translator tools from IDS, an independent conversion tool vendor based in Phoenix, Arizona.

Different Migration Paths

Yes, there is no misprint in the above sentence, Mediply is moving to open systems rather than the proprietary AS/400s mentioned at the start of this section. Mediply's top management team decided several months after signing the initial contract with SIC to change from moving to an IBM AS/400-based distributed system to a UNIX configuration with HP9000 servers. The SIC team was surprised by the quick about-face. All of a sudden in January of 1992, the new CEO of Mediply became an open systems convert and started pressing for the open systems benefits he had read and heard about. "Let's switch away from the AS/400 and reduce our systems cost to half," invoked the CEO in intense internal systems planning meetings, "They say open systems should also raise our development productivity by four times."

Mr. Mickel knew that large savings were achievable when moving from proprietary mainframes to distributed open systems, but doubted a move from proprietary midrange to open midrange systems could provide as much as 50%, at least in the near term. He believed the savings would be there in the longer term, and would stem from greater competition among software and hardware vendors in the open environment. He followed the CEO's guidance and quickly found a set of open systems application packages with equivalent functionality to the package he had planned for the AS/400 platform. The last-minute change of operating system had delayed Mediply's implementation schedule and so Mr. Mickel wasted little time choosing an open systems hardware platform vendor to provide the servers. Since open system surveys Mr. Mickel had read pointed to HP as the appropriate choice for general-purpose UNIX servers, he called on HP to provide the platform for the new system. As Mr. Mickel had expected, the HP platform cost about half the IBM 4381 mainframe and provided greater functionality. He was also pleased that HP was able to provide 10-20% cost savings versus the fully negotiated IBM AS/400 midrange system price.

The main motivation for system change at Mediply, as mentioned earlier, was the need to rid the business of inadequate and burdensome application software and the accompanying expensive hardware platform. Mediply did not view its software as an investment; it was a yearly maintenance drain...an unnecessary cost of doing business.

SIC was thus instructed to rid Mediply of the "spaghetti code" developed over the years. Some of the software was based on packages bought awhile back, such as Culinet's accounts receivable software for IDMS, which had been altered, according to Mr. Mickel, "beyond recognition." Viewing the old software as an expense rather than as an asset has made Mr. Mickel's migration relatively straightforward. He has few worries about backward compatibility as he builds the new system using the new open systems applications for order entry, materials management, inventory control, purchasing, warehousing, and accounts receivable. He plans to run the new and old systems in parallel starting January 1993 (the Florida operations will migrate to the new systems first and then be followed by the rest of the company) and cut off the old system in March. The payroll and general ledger at that point will be the only applications left behind on the mainframe and will either be transferred to SIC for outsourcing or considered for conversion/replacement on the new platform later during 1993. The new platform is to consist of several application, communication, and database UNIX servers linked by T1 lines to over 250 terminals and 100 HP Vectra PCs in the distribution centers and branches.

As is often the case, some application packages cannot be used as-is due to subtle areas of mismatch between the package design and the company's management practices. Mediply's management philosophy is to give sales managers ultimate flexibility on pricing, discounts, and even invoice format so as to effectively position Mediply in every high potential deal. Mr. Mickel staffed up to modify what he estimates to be 5% of the application package code in order to meet this management need. During the transition, he is asking the bulk of Mediply's mainframe software engineers to continue running the existing mainframe. He is placing the four Mediply programmers he feels are most suited to the newer tasks into an "open systems team," and is bringing SIC system engineers and programmers from around the U.S. to help with open systems development.

Since the new application packages are based on the Progress Fourth-Generation Language (4GL), Mr. Mickel does not need to have UNIX and C language experts in his application development teams. The Progress 4GL development tools and relational database shield most of the programmers from having to know about the underlying system software and operating system. This simplification shortens the learning curve for new programmers (one week of training is sufficient) and speeds up system development. To counterbalance the lack of system knowledge in the programmer population, however, Mr. Mickel needs a larger core of expert networking and system management people in his organization to support the rest of the team. He wants to eventually staff the core team at "one and one," one networking specialist and one Progress/UNIX expert. For the time being, however, the work load demands "one and three," one networking expert and three Progress/UNIX gurus.

Mr. Mickel sees the current migration as just the beginning of an evolution toward using information systems for obtaining a strategic advantage in Mediply's business. The new system will be a world apart from the old. It will support three times the data volumes on day one and soon will be linked to suppliers and customers through Electronic Data Interchange (EDI) supporting 40,000 active line items. Managers and staff who carried out manual calculations for this function in the past can apply themselves to more productive work in the sales and marketing organizations. As the system evolves, salespeople will also be able to access the system through notebook PCs and modems from home and in the field, cutting transit time/costs and office space requirements as well.

In the meantime, however, Mr. Mickel is dealing with the difficulties of transitioning to the newer technology. He had a rude awakening when he found that open system software application vendors could not answer what he viewed as relatively straightforward questions for estimating network traffic and CPU load. "They couldn't even provide me with estimates of how many system transactions are generated per customer order," Mr. Mickel remarks. His questions concerning other typical mainframe utilities such as automatic backup and storage, data storage recovery, check-pointing, and roll-forward and roll-back recovery were also met with blank stares and unsatisfactory answers. The vendors claimed that customers had rarely asked such questions. He soon found the reason why; more often than not their previous customers had been upsizers from PC networks with little mainframe experience.

After the initial shock, Mr. Mickel recovered and then rethought his approach; rather than ask for functionality that existed on the mainframe, he worked with the vendors to develop a system management environment that takes advantage of the benefits of both worlds. On the whole, he is now comfortable with the results of his joint efforts with the system and application vendors. His program will give him a workable solution with superior cost advantages. Nevertheless, he sees considerable development work in his future as he builds in the commercial robustness that his computing environment demands. He feels somewhat relieved by HP's ability to help him along the way.

As mentioned above, Ian Inman at Delight is taking a different migration path from Mediply. His first step is not to replace the software, but to restructure and re-engineer the 1.3 million lines of code, including 1,700 programs and 600 screens, to the open systems platform. Software adjustments already scheduled as part of ongoing maintenance, such as changing date parameters to the year 2000, are to be undertaken at the same time. Once the conversion is completed the management team will then select candidate applications for "open systems" enhancement or, in some cases, replacement by newer application package solutions running in the open systems environment.

Mr. Inman is not choosing this path because he or the management team is enamored of the old code. Many of the older batch systems have not been substantially updated since 1965, and do not meet today's requirements. He sees less urgency in going for wholesale replacement at Delight because the business is less information intensive than Mediply's. Delight deals with a smaller number of product lines and fewer direct customers.

The sequenced approach Mr. Inman has chosen to follow allows him to spend more time ensuring that he selects the best software on which to bet Delight's future business. Moving off the mainframe itself, however, can't wait.

Mr. Inman calculated the difference between using internal MIS staff to migrate off the mainframe over a four-year period versus employing an outside migration specialist, IDS, to complete the job in six months. He expects an internal team would take more time due to staffing constraints, unavoidable learning curves, and the need to make do without some of the specialist conversion tools available to IDS. His calculations show that unplugging the main-frame more than three years ahead of time provides savings of $336,000 in maintenance and $126,000 in lease costs versus having the systems coexist over that period of time. Add to that the avoid-ance of a costly $150,000 functionality enhancement to the main-frame (moving to an open operating system)—a necessary expense if the mainframe system is to be operated concurrently with the newer open systems—and the savings total $610,000, well exceeding the IDS $400,000 bill for migration services. He adds that the savings are even greater if the "intangibles" of having his staff freed up over the three-year period are included. He mentally calculates these intangibles as, "Assuming an internal migration effort would con-sume one-third of our people over four years...freeing them up could translate into an additional $800,000 of programming time we can invest in open systems enhancements." Mr. Inman now has plans in place to be completely off the mainframe by November of 1993.

Which software will be enhanced first? Mr. Inman expects that will depend on which areas will provide the greatest near-term busi-ness benefits. Improving market forecasting and revenue projection capabilities are of the highest interest to Delight's management team. They feel that more accurate forecasts will reduce inventory expenses, a major cost factor of Delight's business. Mr. Inman has already taken steps toward importing data from IRI, a POS retail information provider, and installing software for analyzing the data to support a more reliable forecasting methodology. He expects the first application packages installed will be financial and accounting programs since most of the popular packages for these functions meet all the standard reporting requirements. The second set will probably be in manufacturing, where Mr. Inman expects he will need to work with the management team to re-engineer parts of the pro-cesses before moving ahead with a new set of packages.

Mr. Inman's "move off and then replace" migration strategy has also provided him more flexibility in migrating his IS staff. When Mr. Mickel at Mediply pulls the plug on the mainframe next year, his staff will be surrounded by a completely new set of systems and applications...and so will Mediply's business managers. When Delight pulls the plug, the MIS team will at least be working with the same applications. Mr. Inman believes his more gradual migration path will allow him to avoid losing staff in the transition. He is encouraging his staff to build skills for the new environment, and has scheduled training for all of them in UNIX, system administration, Oracle database, and CASE tools, at a cost of less than "half of one person's annual salary and benefits."

Mr. Inman has already trained several of his staff members in PC development and administration. A senior PC program analyst in his organization says he is happy to be off the mainframe. He has attended three PC training courses and is already putting in place a PC LAN infrastructure to convert 120 Delight users (especially those requiring frequent reports) to PCs running Netware, Word for Windows, and E-mail, over the next six months. The PC program analyst comments, "They should be happy to get their reports immediately on request with the PCs. Up until now with the mainframe, a report took six to eight months. I know, I used to generate them."

The Tricky Question of Moving the Software

Hey! What about the 20-30 years worth of code on the mainframe? Good question. If you put this question to companies who have downsized or to their consultants, you might be perplexed by the answer you get. Larry DeBoever of DeBoever Architectures Technologies, an IS architecture consulting firm based in Acton, Massachusetts, may inform you that your old software code is NOT an asset, but an EXPENSE to doing business. He will say the longer you stay with outdated code the farther you will fall behind your downsizing competition. An MIS manager who recently downsized and opted to leave his mainframe software behind remarked, "Isn't it funny that hardware from 20 years ago is in the Smithsonian Museum and software from that same era is running on the mainframe at many companies tonight?" At the same time, there are just as many managers who feel the opposite, i.e., that it is best to keep the software intact, and take on the task of migrating their mainframe code to UNIX platforms. Thanks to the barrage of new tools and techniques for making the move, this path has become much more feasible, especially for companies operating in the most standard mainframe environments.

Holding on to the Mainframe Software

Much to the dismay of many UNIX purists, it is possible to run Cobol programs on UNIX. It is also now possible to port applications that were created using mainframe development tools that have since found their way to the UNIX environment, such as IBI's FOCUS and Software AG's Natural. What do you get for doing that? Well, how about lower operating cost and a more flexible environment? Migrating companies cannot obtain as many of these benefits as complete downsizers using C language programs and UNIX applications. Nevertheless, substantial improvements are reported by companies opting for this route. Let's quickly review the list of reasons companies give for holding onto mainframe software:

- **Protect Assets:** These companies have found significant business advantages from the custom code developed for their systems, or the mainframe applications they have used over the years. They want to avoid having to redevelop the same software on a new platform and also want to forego retraining their users on new applications.

- **Minimize Variables:** Some companies have decided that changing hardware and software at the same time is too risky and difficult to manage. It is difficult to tell, for instance, whether a system crash was caused by a faulty circuit board or a missing software subroutine. Keeping the deltas to a minimum by only changing the hardware platform at first allows MIS organizations to focus their energies on a smaller set of important transition issues. This is viewed as extremely important by many MIS shops short on staff with experience in the new environment.

- **Convince the Skeptics:** The type of inertia that can build up in many MIS shops is well-illustrated by the stories in this book. In an environment where nay-sayers abound, it sometimes make sense to have a small controllable win before taking on the whole move. By minimizing variables during the transition, there is less chance of encountering short-term setbacks which are inevitably leveraged by the opposing camp to stop the project. If the small win is substantial and credible enough, it might even convert the skeptics into downsizing supporters.

- **If It Ain't Broke, Don't Fix It:** Many MIS managers won't even allow system upgrades into their computer environment. They have been stung too many times by tapes from the vendor that add extra functions, and just as often as not, contain bugs that dismantle an instruction set critical for business applications unique to their environment. When these managers look at migration options available to them, in their minds, they see bugs...lots of intractable bugs they could spend months fixing to get the system running again. These individuals are more likely to opt for leaving the code as-is on the mainframe and surrounding it with front- and back-end systems to enhance response time and add flexibility.

There are many reasons for holding onto software, of which the above are most often cited. Whatever the reason for keeping your software, however, there are fundamentally three ways for making the move (listed below). Using these migration methods in combination is also possible and often done.

1. **Follow the Software Vendor:** If the software vendor who developed your mainframe application package has ported it to UNIX, you are in luck. Usually all you have to do is buy the new package and you are off and running on the new platform.

2. **Convert:** Software companies have come to the rescue with conversion tools for moving custom code as-is from the most common mainframe environments to UNIX.

3. **Surround:** This is also called the "wolf pack" strategy. The idea is to place several UNIX servers in the divisions, usually equipped with relational database software and some UNIX application packages, so that files can be periodically downloaded from the mainframe (or mainframes) and made accessible to users linked up to the servers. It is called the "wolf pack" because once a significant number of servers are brought on board, all the data and applications find their way down to the wolves (servers) and there is little for the mainframe to munch on, and thus, little reason for its expensive existence. Cambridge Technology Group, an IT consulting and system integration company, uses this term, "surround," to describe the approach they often recommend for their customers.

Application Packages Already Downsized

So which mainframe software vendors are moving their applications to UNIX? A large number of the major ones. Let me discuss a few and then list some others that are relatively well known.

Dun & Bradstreet (D&B): D&B owns 60% of the mainframe financial applications marketplace in the U.S., boasts a similarly dominant position in most of Europe, and has a strong presence in the Asia/Pacific region. They have 12,000 customers worldwide, and they are carefully monitoring the expectations of these customers with respect to downsizing. At this point, according to Bobby

Cameron, D&B's director of product management for advanced technologies, 18% of their customers are actively downsizing, basically to save money; another 38% are expecting to gain more from downsizing than just cost reduction and are investing in re-engineering their business by installing client/server systems. The remaining 44% are either in the investigation stage or "asleep" with respect to downsizing. Nevertheless, Mr. Cameron believes that virtually all of D&B's customer base will wake up to downsizing and client/server over the next two years.

To serve this customer base effectively, D&B has embarked on two major programs: a software migration (moving the well-known Millenium family of mainframe and VAX products to UNIX) and a software development program that not only brings mainframe applications to the downsized environment (D&B's family of more than 26 applications are being re-engineered from a "clean sheet of paper" to form the SmartStream family of products), but also makes use of the advantages inherent to the client/server environment.

SmartStream's decision support is an example of these re-engineered products for the downsized environment. It provides access, analysis, distribution, presentation, and development/application services via a Microsoft Windows client and an SQL server. The accessed information can reside on internal databases or in external data services. Information residing within other D&B applications is especially compatible.

Computer Associates (CA): CA, the largest software vendor in the U.S., with over $1 billion in mainframe software revenues, is on the move as well. Their chairman and chief executive, Charles B. Wang, commented to a group of journalists that "the UNIX market has become as important to CA as the mainframe market." The multitude of companies depending on CA's system management software to manage workload, data storage, performance monitoring, and security on their mainframes may be happy to know that CA has ported its full suite of CA-UNICENTER management tools to the UNIX environment. CA's other applications, such as IDMS, Datacom, Masterpiece, and financial tools are also being moved over as this book goes to press.

Information Builders Inc. (IBI): IBI is the vendor of FOCUS fourth-generation language (4GL) development tools used by approximately 20% of mainframe shops. IBI has a strategic partnership with IBM to develop and market IBI's DB2 database access tools (EDA) for what

IBM calls their "Information Warehouse Strategy." This product, as well as others, including FOCUS, are available on UNIX today and supported by dedicated IBI UNIX platform sales representatives.

As mentioned above, many other software houses are taking the plunge to open systems. Table 5-1 is a list of some of the better known companies by software category.

Table 5-1: Open Systems Software

Category	SW Vendor	Application
Financials/ Human Resources	Computer Associates International, Inc.	Masterpiece
	Cyborg	Payroll, Time & Attendance
	Dun & Bradstreet	Millenium SmartStream*
	Lawson Associates	Human Resource Accounting System
	Oracle	Oracle Financials
	SAP	SAP R/3*
Manufacturing/ Logistics	Andersen Consulting	FMD
	American Software	
	Brock	Brock Control Systems
	Cincom	Control
	Dun & Bradstreet	AMAPS
	Lawson Associates	Distribution System
	Manugistics	
	SAP	SAP R/3*
	Xerox Computer Services	CHESS
Executive Information Services	SAS	SAS
	Pilot Executive	Pilot EIS
	Information Builders, Inc.	FOCUS
	IRI	EXPRESS
Systems Management	Computer Associates International, Inc.	CA-UNICENTER*

Table 5-1: Open Systems Software (Continued)

Category	SW Vendor	Application
DBMS/4GLs/ CASE	Computer Associates International, Inc.	IDMS
		Datacom
		Ideal
	CGI	PacBase
		PacLan
	Cincom Systems, Inc.	Supra
		Mantis
	Information Builders, Inc.	FOCUS
	IRI	EXPRESS
	Oracle	Oracle Tools
	SoftLab	Maestro II
	Software AG Systems Inc.	Adabas
		Natural
	Texas Instruments Incorporated	IEF

*   indicates new products developed specifically for the UNIX environment, not just ported
     mainframe software.

There has also been late-breaking news about IBM porting its CICS mainframe transaction processing environment to the IBM RS6000 UNIX platform. On September 22, 1992, IBM also announced porting of the CICS environment to HP-UX platforms. Over 80% of installed mainframes world-wide are estimated to have CICS/Cobol programs installed, and so this port is expected to lay the foundation for a landslide of migrations.

Moving to Ported Applications

Those readers who have found their application packages on the above list may be asking the next question. Just how easy is it (really) to use these ported applications? Let's quickly go through the steps for porting and list the caveats.

- **Switching to UNIX versions of traditional mainframe application software** is fairly straightforward. After purchasing the new UNIX version of say, Pilot's EIS or a SAS analysis package, the mainframe data needs to be migrated. This is done by extracting the data from the mainframe database, whether it be in hierarchical or relational format, as a flat or "holding" file. The data is then converted through TCP/IP utilities from EBCIDIC IBM mainframe code to ASCII, the data code for most desktop systems and servers, and transferred to the new UNIX platform. Some final formatting adjustments need to be carried out to define record lengths and other database parameters before settling the data into its new database (usually relational) home on the server. This final formatting only requires a small amount of straightforward programming according to those experienced with the process.

- **Moving applications developed in a transported 4GL environment over to a new UNIX platform** is slightly more complex. Not all of the database structures and languages that the mainframe 4GLs work with are transportable. Often, parts of the trustworthy mainframe applications developed by MIS will have to be rewritten. What are the steps for this type of conversion? Let's take applications using IBI's FOCUS tools as an example.

1. Take stock of the applications residing on the mainframe today and identify those written in the FOCUS environment. Since FOCUS programs are written for such commonly required tasks as extracting data, writing reports, and maintaining records, they can be found attached to virtually any mainframe activity that generates or summarizes data. It is not uncommon for FOCUS users to have thousands of these programs running on their mainframe platforms.

2. Determine which FOCUS programs are necessary in the new environment. Applications should be categorized by function, content, database links, input/output requirements, difficulty of conversion, business value (even a subjective ranking here is okay), etc. The difficulty of conversion, as mentioned above, often corresponds to the degree the FOCUS program relies on database structures and languages that cannot follow it to the new environment. Some examples of non-transferable languages are: Assembler, PL/1, XEDIT, REXX, and variations of Cobol. Since these parts need to be rewritten, MIS departments may want to slate applications with these encumbrances for

later conversion (after MIS members have become used to the more routine aspects of downsizing), or may choose to replace them with UNIX programs that fulfill similar roles. It may also be prudent for the MIS department to choose applications related to only one set of business activities (say accounting) for the first go-round, and then branch out to the remaining programs on a second run.

3. Run the candidate FOCUS programs in what is referred to as a "cleansed" environment as a precautionary check to see if you have really identified all of the dependencies for each program. Leaving behind a linked subroutine, for instance, will crash the transported program on the new system and MIS staff may have difficulty determining whether the cause is faulty hardware or incomplete software. To conduct the cleansed environment test, place all the related subroutines and databases for the candidate FOCUS program on one disk, detach the other disks and run the program. If it does not generate error messages and completes its tasks appropriately, chances are the application is complete.

4. Transport the program code over using a process similar to the migration process for data described above. Use TCP/IP's file transfer protocol (FTP) to move the program code and associated data across TCP/IP links to the new UNIX platform.

5. Minor clean-up is usually required to get the applications humming again (at hopefully even faster speeds on the new platform). UNIX systems, for instance, are much more case-sensitive than their mainframe cousins. They require all commands and file names to be represented in lowercase letters.

The degree to which the transfer process goes smoothly also depends somewhat on the environment itself. The MIS director at a well-known computer research organization downsized applications developed in both FOCUS and Oracle environments. The upshot from his experience was that Oracle compatibility was excellent across all platforms. With the FOCUS programs, however, he felt as though he was on the "bleeding edge" of a new technology, running into problems even the software vendor had not fully anticipated. Nevertheless, he completed his mission, downsized to HP-UX servers (four production servers and one development server) and unplugged the mainframe.

These FOCUS weaknesses may be short-lived. IBI has taken them to heart and is addressing them ASAP.

Convert!

But what about those applications and environments which have not been ported by software vendors to the new environment yet? What about the CICS/Cobol programs that can't wait for the ported IBM CICS versions? Three software vendors offer different ways to bring CICS/Cobol off the mainframe to UNIX platforms. With each vendor, there are different challenges and requirements, as well as a different set of end-products. It is important to check them out fully before moving ahead. Here are some brief summaries of the "How To's" for each vendor.

- **VISystems** (CICS Functional requests converted to VIS/TP Calls): VISystems is one of the first pioneers in the CICS/Cobol conversion field. In addition to CICS/Cobol programs, VISystem tools also convert VSAM files to the new environment.

  As indicated in the above parentheses, the VISystems methodology converts CICS functional requests into VIS/TP management interface calls, and VSAM database files to "VIS/VSAM" format, both appropriate for UNIX. The converted programs are compiled in C, a language native to the UNIX environment. Even after conversion, the applications retain the capability of accessing the DL/1 database on the mainframe through DL/1 commands issued across the network.

  Companies who are not yet comfortable making adjustments to programs in C language or using C code generating 4GLs for program maintenance and upgrading, have the option with VISystems tools of transporting the code back to the mainframe for reworking by their mainframe-experienced staff. The revised code can then be downloaded back to the UNIX platform. This type of arduous conversion, of course, defeats most of the reasons for moving to a new more flexible and efficient platform. Back and forth maintenance conversion is only recommended for the very initial stages, while MIS team members are cutting their teeth on the new UNIX tools.

- **CONVEYOR** (CICS screens converted to CURSES with run-time modules): CONVEYOR is a tool developed by InfoSoft (a German Company) and marketed and distributed in the U.S. by Innovative Information Systems (IISI) and Wesson Taylor Wells (WTW). The CONVEYOR tool mimics CICS capabilities with CURSES-based screen forms and run-time modules to carry out such functions as on-line data, form, queue, and pipeline access, as well as printer control. The mainframe Cobol portion is converted to MicroFocus Cobol for the UNIX environment through automatic conversion tools and utilities.

- **UNIKIX** (conversion with little source code modification): UNIKIX is developed and distributed by the systems integration arm of Groupe Bull. UNIKIX's compatibility with commonly-used CICS commands and its high-level implementation of CICS application binary interface allow for easy porting and minimum source code modification. Mainframe Cobol applications using the commands supported by UNIKIX are fully source-compatible and will operate the same way on UNIX. UNIKIX also supplies porting utilities for converting Cobol programs to UNIX-based MicroFocus Cobol.

UNIKIX developers also invested in making it comfortable for downsizing companies in transition. VSAM mainframe database files can either be emulated on the UNIX platform or left on the mainframe and accessed through the traditional IBM SNA networks. UNIKIX provides PU4 and PU5 protocols allowing UNIKIX programs and end users with, say, ASCII terminals, to simultaneously access UNIX and CICS applications and use data from databases that are local, on other parts of the network, and on the mainframe.

In addition to tools for converting from Cobol/CICS, there are also versions for porting from various Unisys mainframes. The Unisys tools, for the most part, vary by the type of system being offloaded.

- Unisys A and V series systems (previously Burroughs systems): Openware Technologies Inc.provides a MicroXGen software 4GL to convert Unisys LINC and XGEN programs over. Openware also delivers tools for A and V series Cobol program conversion to MicroFocus Cobol

- Unisys 1100 and 2200 systems (previously Sperry systems): Zortec's tools convert Unisys Mapper and Cobol applications to Zortec's System Z 4GL, which runs on UNIX.

- Unisys System 80s: Allinson Ross provides a TIP/ix tool for converting TIP/30 applications to TIP/ix running on UNIX

More recently a new variety of tools is being introduced from DenKart, Plexus, and IDS which are claimed to support migration from any environment to any environment. These tools use an expert system methodology by which a knowledge base (rules and logical data tables) is created for the source and target environments. Programs written in the source language are then converted over through a reiterative process to the target language, allowing the system to "learn" the full rules of conversion during the migration process. Data tables and databases are converted using a similar methodology with logical tables that take into account the complexity of data account relationships inherent to the two environments.

Surround the Mainframe

Companies preferring to stay on the mainframe, but also wanting to obtain the flexibility and data access advantages of distributed relational databases, simply need to install servers, load relational database software, such as Oracle, INFORMIX, Sybase, etc. on the servers, define the type of data files to periodically download, choose the desktop devices to be used for accessing and/or inputting the data, install a network with links to the mainframe database, and start rolling! It is not, of course, as easy as that, but certainly the lack of a need to convert applications makes it a lot simpler (the implementation steps mentioned here are described in more detail in Chapters 6 and 7). Since the mainframe is to remain in use indefinitely, MIS shops taking this approach cannot usually justify the "downsizing" program through cost savings. That is, of course, unless the system permits the company to avoid upgrading the mainframe, and the incremental costs for the new surrounding network amounts to less than the price of an upgrade. Instead, surround strategies are typically justified by a business case analysis emphasizing the benefits derived from bringing information closer to the decision-makers in the company, or for instance, enhanced customer service due to easier access to customer data at the desktop of the service representative.

What to Do If You Don't Want to Keep Your Mainframe Software

End-user frustration with the limited functionality of old mainframe application packages and custom software developed for a different era, or for a different business, may have reached an all-time high at your company. Users may, in fact, be overjoyed at the prospect of being trained on one of the newer easy-to-use graphical user interface packages that coordinate the activities of newer paradigm packages to transport data on request, create reports automatically, bring new expertise to problem-solving, etc. MIS staff may also be ready for the productivity improvements provided by reusable code, parallel team development, and 4GL CASE tools that automatically generate code. Companies with these types of constituencies do not usually want to hassle with the migration efforts and code incompatibility issues described in the last section to "just run the same old code a little faster and cheaper." They want to break away from the past and gain all of the efficiencies and advantages open systems and distributed topologies can provide. Typically these companies are looking to:

- Forget about past sunk costs. They recognize that MIS staff spent years developing the mainframe code, but they also see that it is not serving the needs of the business. They also expect it would take much longer (and be more costly on an ongoing basis) to revise the old code than to bring in new application packages and adjust them.

- Apply the new technology to business problems that help the company gain a competitive advantage, whether it be super-efficient customer service, paperless order entry through delivery systems, zero-inventory-control systems, decision-support systems, or some other capability other competitors haven't thought of, or haven't installed yet.

- Ensure that none of the extra mainframe baggage—e.g., needless proprietary code emulators, outdated system management tools for preserving MIPs and memory—is brought into the new environment.

Companies that might want to opt for one of the conversion strategies mentioned earlier, may also find themselves joining the ranks of these aggressive movers simply because their current mainframe application package vendor has not moved its mainframe software applications to the new distributed environment. If, for instance, your mainframe runs PROFS or COPICS, you may fall into this category.

Companies with dyed-in-the-wool mainframe applications need to move to new systems either by replacing their mainframe applications with equivalent UNIX packages, or by rewriting the packages with open systems 4GLs and other development tools.

Go Ahead and Replace It

Finding an effective replacement for current applications is not an easy task. The marketing messages and demos provided by software vendors can often be misleading to first-time viewers of the software. Applications and tools usually appear much easier to install, program, and use than is actually the case, and the functionality often seems more abundant in the demo than when it is up and running in the office, where seasoned users try to squeeze specific data requests out of the system.

The approach used at many companies, including American Airlines, is to assign joint user/MIS task forces to assess the various types of software available on the market (within certain guidelines determined by MIS, such as operating system and networking compatibility) and come up with a short list of final candidates. The final candidates get thoroughly tested for reliability, compatibility, scalability, etc., and those that pass become certified as "acceptable software" for the company. Limiting company desktop software to specific types and versions eases the system management job considerably, especially if the network is large enough to warrant conducting server and client software updates from a central location. In a standardized environment, system problems can be more quickly diagnosed and resolved because there are fewer variables to consider.

The software houses who are simply porting their software packages "as is" from the mainframe environment may not be suitable candidates for aggressive downsizing companies who, as mentioned above, want to leave excess mainframe baggage behind...but that does not mean that all purveyors of traditional mainframe applications should be shunned. Many of these companies, including the previously mentioned Dun & Bradstreet are adjusting their offerings and creating new applications to take full advantage of the distributed and client/server environments.

German-based SAP is an example of a software application company making the full transformation to client/server. SAP has become the dominant player in the mainframe enterprise-wide integrated systems market in Europe and is also a strong force in the U.S. SAP software provides a common database with application interfaces that allow the financial, marketing, sales, and engineering organizations to all work from and share the same data. SAP was among the first major software vendors to announce a complete rewrite of a popular mainframe package (SAP's R/2) for the client/server market. The re-engineered R/3 version is available in Europe, the U.S., and Japan.

Peoplesoft is an example of a software company growing rapidly toward a leadership position in the market due to their early move to the client/server. Peoplesoft's human resource package enables easy access and superior text and graphic filing, presentation, and formatting capabilities for personnel and administration departments. It helps these departments keep up not only with the demands of managing and motivating employees, but also with the myriad government reports expanding in volume and complexity every year.

It's Easier Than you Might Think to Rewrite

Many companies find that their business requires something special from their information system that is not supplied by any of the application packages available. Liteline, for instance, was surprised to find that no packages allowed them to price their product lines by promotion rather than by product. Having to adjust each product line separately during frequent promotions of ladies' attire and exercise outfits would have been a step backward in productivity for Liteline. A rewrite was their only option.

This option may not be as burdensome as many MIS mainframe veterans have come to expect from painful past experiences. Rewriting has come a long way with the help of 4GLs, prototyping, rapid application development technology, etc. Let me first describe some of the past methodologies and then contrast them with options available in the open systems environment today.

It is estimated that approximately 70% of the in-house developed Cobol programs running on mainframes today were hand-coded in Cobol without 4GLs or CASE tools. When the development efforts for these programs were structured (rather than developed through informal interaction among individuals), the methodology was often what is referred to as "waterfall," with six sequential phases. First came the pre-requirement scoping of the program objectives and resources, then a more detailed assessment of requirements and analysis of the program components involved. Afterward, the components were incorporated into a full application design, and the design was coded. The final development phase included the testing and integration of the various developed components, and the integration of the program itself with other applications on the mainframe. Ongoing maintenance of the application code was included as an activity of the final phase.

The phased waterfall approach was first implemented with fairly strict sequencing. Developers were not allowed to go back and correct deficiencies in prior phases without a very good reason. When it was realized, however, that allowing iterations among phases would improve the application fit with user and business needs (many coming to the team's attention during the process), development teams began to allow the waterfall to flow back uphill. This led to a development structure called the "spiral" approach. Spiral teams were given the freedom to back up one (and only one) phase to correct serious oversights and missed opportunities. Backing up any further, it was thought, would delay the program too much, endangering deadline commitments, and in some cases putting the whole project at risk. Spiral projects appeared to deliver higher quality programs and meet user needs better, but there were definite limits to the extent that user-required functionality could be incorporated. Development schedules, originally set in months, more often than not took years to complete. Often the business requirements that prompted the development program had changed significantly by the time applications were finally started up. Sometimes new applications were rendered obsolete on day one.

Overview of Development Productivity Tools and Methodologies

The first tools introduced for software development made portions of the sequential development processes more efficient. Today these are referred to as *Stand-alone CASE tools*, which are still effective for small informal development teams who interact constantly throughout the development process to coordinate their activities. These are lower CASE tools, for the most part, including 3GLs, 4GLs, editors, and debuggers, which address the back-end code generation and editing stages of the development process. They are also useful for customizing off-the-shelf applications for which the basic structure of the application has already been defined.

Open integrated and *Integrated CASE tools* were later developed to take on the additional coordination challenges of larger project teams working on the same application, sometimes in geographically disparate locations. Open integrated CASE tools are sets of loosely integrated development tools, each designed to address a different portion of the development process. Users can choose from a set of compatible tools to be "encapsulated" by the tool environment's linkage software. Once encapsulated, the tools work as an integrated whole, providing for automatic communication and control across project teams working in tandem on different development phases.

Code generation tools and development databases (repositories) are generally not included, and would be difficult to implement in this "mix and match" environment.

The code generation and repository functions are integral parts, however, of *Integrated CASE Tools (I-CASE)* which address the needs of the largest, most complex programs for which ongoing maintenance is of high concern. I-CASE tools provide integrated toolsets for each part of the development life cycle from prerequisites to maintenance (even re-engineering). Parallel development activities are closely coordinated via a central repository responsible for registering all global data, sharing data among development phases, and controlling all application changes.

Which tools do you think are best? Unfortunately, factors in addition to functionality come into play when deciding on CASE tools, any of which can undermine an otherwise effective CASE tool implementation program.

- The more integrated CASE tools control the development processes so rigorously that an unpopular reorganization of the development group is often required to use them appropriately
- The more senior developers often balk at the prospect of casting their years of development experience to the wind in favor of a new-fangled set of tools that are untried at their company
- Consulting expenses are sometimes necessary to see the first efforts off to a good start
- The cost of the more sophisticated integrated CASE tools can appear exorbitant (as much as $50,000 per developer)

Nevertheless, MIS shops looking into downsizing are considering both the loosely integrated (HP's Softbench is an example), and fully integrated (TI's IEF tools are an example) for transitioning their MIS staff to the new environment. As mentioned in the description of Bill Williams' plans at Liteline, he expects not to have to train his people in C because he feels he can depend on the 4GL from TI to generate code accurately. When the reduced training costs and the added ease of development are factored in, $50,000 per developer may not be as bad as it sounds.

Product Development Methodologies

Product development methodologies that leverage these newer CASE tool technologies are also evolving, especially those for accurately incorporating user needs into the early phases of the development process. *Prototyping* is becoming popular because it allows users to experience what the new application will be like at the outset and to provide more accurate feedback for use in early design changes. Without prototyping, the potential for misunderstandings between users and developers far outweighs the probability of getting everything right, or even nearly right. Prototyping also allows programmers to test how the application works before adding encumbering overhead, such as error handling, help menus, and security.

The second methodology, *Rapid Application Development (RAD)* is an outgrowth of the I-CASE tool environment. These tools are used in RAD programs to generate entire applications with minimal to no hand programming. Integral to the RAD process is the establishing of ongoing joint user/developer workshops. Early in the process, JRP (Joint Requirements Planning) sessions are held including executives, end users, and IS professionals to define requirements for the system under development. JAD (Joint Application Development) workshops are then conducted regularly to develop and evolve the program design specifications. The much higher level of end-user involvement helps resolve many of the user frustration issues of the earlier development approaches, and the I-CASE technologies speed up development time considerably. With RAD, applications that satisfy end users are being completed before the business requirements change!

Is System Development Becoming Simpler or More Difficult?

Confusing Worlds

Two types of confusion are highlighted by the experts. Similar sounding terms can have completely different meanings, and completely different terms can represent similar notions. Michael Bauer, Technology Architecture Manager at EDS, the systems integration giant based in Plano, Texas, claims that much of the confusion surrounding distributed computing and client/server systems can be blamed on jargon. He says that VSAM and ISAM, for instance, both exist in the mainframe world and stand for file types. SAM without the preceding "V" or "I" exists in the downsized, open systems environment but may refer to an HP system management tool, a completely different function. Larry DeBoever of DeBoever Architectures Technologies, likes to point out that some of the jargon mix-ups may be a conspiracy. He views the downsized, client/server world as, in large part, a repackaging of many traditional mainframe computing concepts to look "new" through the use of different names..."a new church Latin." He gives an example of how cross-memory services in MVS use approximately the same format as a "Named Pipes" call across the network to a distributed database.

Other misunderstandings, according to Mr. Bauer, stem from applying mainframe economics to the new distributed world. Mainframe systems were designed to effectively manage the most expensive computing resources of the mainframe era: CPU cycles and memory. Consequently, system software was developed to share one CPU across vast organizations and push the frontiers of minimal memory use. IBM's CICS transaction processing environment was developed, for instance, to re-use database connections. Instead of having to reserve transaction memory for every user on the system, CICS allows 100 users to work with 6 memory areas and database connections. The memory and CPU savings of 6 vs. 100 in the mainframe environment are substantial. The economics have changed, however, according to George Schussel, editor of a journal issued in his own name on downsizing. He says that massive reductions in price per MIPS (Millions of Instructions Per Second) and TPS (Transactions Per Second) created by advances in RISC-based UNIX workstations and PCs, make CPU cost insignificant. At an August 1992 Downsizing Expo in San Francisco, he summed up his perspectives with one memorable announcement, "MIPS are free!" Mr. Bauer observes that similar savings have occurred in disk storage to drive the costs below $3.00 per megabyte. So what is expensive in the computing environment today? People time, according to Mr. Bauer, whether they be MIS staff developing software applications or end users generating reports from corporate data. As MIS departments leave the world of expensive MIPS and enter an era of expensive people, it may be worthwhile checking if all the excess mainframe baggage, in both hardware and system software, has been left behind. This is not an easy task. It requires scrutinizing the tools MIS used in the old environment and asking tough questions about the suitability of each one under the new constraints and opportunities. To do this requires keeping up with the open systems game. MIS managers must know enough about distributed environments to match their needs with the capabilities of countless open systems tools and utilities making their debuts with every issue of *PC WEEK*.

A final area of confusion, according to Mr. Bauer, is a mismatch of older paradigm expectations with newer paradigm realities. He was surprised at a recent engineering and research conference to hear a lab manager complaining that he had to reboot a new UNIX system every week, versus almost never with the prior mainframe system. A few questions later, Mr. Bauer found out the reason. The research lab had opened up the UNIX system to unlimited access by engineers throughout the site, to experiment with the open systems platform virtually as they wished. Misconstructed code, inappropriate commands, inadequate memory management controls, etc., input by any user could bring down the system. This differed greatly from the limited access provided users in the mainframe environment. Mr. Bauer expects that a mainframe subjected to a similar level of user access would need to be rebooted at least as often.

The above three areas of misunderstanding, jargon, economics, and mismatched expectations, have serious implications for the migrating MIS team that stretch far beyond the redefinition of a term here, and the avoidance of a conceptual pitfall there. The MIS team now needs to discard much of what was taken for granted in running a mainframe shop and reconstruct the computing environment using new terms and tools. They are also subject to new economic priorities and constraints, many of which impact unfamiliar parts of the system previously locked away in the high-security vault called the mainframe.

Simply pondering the challenge, however, will not get us much closer to satisfying the recalcitrant users who have heard that the data they have been refused for years is finally becoming available... or pleasing the management team who has heard that MIS budgets can be cut in half through downsizing. As you may have sensed from the downsizing descriptions up to this point, although the new system topologies are complex and unfamiliar, many MIS managers are finding that the learning experience is not as painful as they expected. The first step is to focus on understanding what exists today in the new environment and taking a shot at constructing a new topology. Once that hurdle is overcome, the light appears at the end of the tunnel, and the road toward downsizing becomes more secure.

First Steps for Constructing a New Paradigm System

To gain a better understanding of what the light at the end of the tunnel looks like, take a moment to consider the major decisions involved in constructing a distributed network topology for moving away from a typical host/terminal environment. As we do so, keep the following set of typical host/terminal issues in mind and ensure they are resolved to your satisfaction during the process:

- Loss of productivity caused by central host down-time impacting the whole company

- Computing bottlenecks, slowing response time to a crawl during peak use periods, due to excessive demands placed on a single host CPU and the overflow of data traffic related to those demands

- Extensive training, including a seemingly endless need for end-user refresher courses due to cryptic ASCII terminal user interfaces. Users are forced to learn difficult-to-remember computer instructions to accomplish otherwise straightforward tasks

Many of the fundamental characteristics of distributed computing itself help address these haunting mainframe world issues. The impact of a failing CPU is mitigated simply by having more than one CPU in the topology. If one goes down, the damage is limited to only the portion of the company served by that particular CPU. Having more than one CPU also allows for high availability options, such as automatic switching of a mission-critical application from one server to the next in the event of a failure. Excessively slow response times and networking bottlenecks are also avoided by distributing the computing burden among many pieces of equipment, and limiting network traffic to essential cross-system calls. The need for training and retraining can also be minimized in the distributed environment through the use of user-friendly graphical user interfaces, powered by intelligent desktop client devices. Simply moving to a distributed client/server environment brings us a long way toward resolving most of the above problems. Let's explore alternative avenues for going further and building the distributed and client/server topology that is most effective for you. Here are six important decision points for guiding us through the alternatives:

1. A relational database?

2. An open systems server?

3. What type of client?

4. How to tie it all together?

5. How to manage the network?

6. Which hardware vendor to choose?

1. A Relational Database?

The need to provide users throughout the company with access to corporate data is often the driving factor for moving to distributed computing. The evolution of database technology to the relational model has made much of this possible.

The early flat file databases, often still found on mainframes, were constructed for massive data storage, not for easy retrieval. Using the flat file hierarchical design, data is arranged starting from one predetermined entry point, say customer name, through which all other related data entries, such as address, products purchased, etc., are accessed. Searches are time-consuming because every file needs to be accessed in sequential order, entry point-by-entry point. With a database organized by customer name, for instance, it would take an excessively long time to obtain a list of customers who ordered a specific part. Even if the list included less than one percent of the total customer base, every customer file would need to be searched sequentially by the computer to develop the final summary.

The next generation of flat file databases were called network model databases. They included a partial work-around to this problem. With networked databases, multiple points of entry could be identified when designing the database files, and used later for data access. If, for instance, the part information in the above example had been marked as an entry point, the list of customers purchasing a certain part could be easily retrieved. The drawback to this model, of course, is the difficulty of anticipating data requirements for all future reports when constructing the original database. The type of data required next week is difficult to predict in today's rapidly fluctuating environment, much less two or three years from today.

During the 1980s, relational model databases appeared and took much of the U.S. market by storm. Two relational database vendors, INFORMIX and Unify, have also grown rapidly in Japan (Oracle is catching up quickly as well), providing large fortunes to Japanese distribution partners (such as ASCII) along the way. The primary advantage of the relational model is that it allows for virtually any on-demand cut of the database. There are no predetermined entry points, data paths, or sequences. The user identifies parameters for cutting the data in SQL language and the database does the rest. It links data tables, summarizes data according to query parameters, returns reports, etc. With the new relational model, databases have been transformed from impenetrable masses of numbers into responsive pools of information waiting to service requests.

Relational database software, however, cannot be responsive without considerable underlying processing power. The advances in inexpensive and high-powered RISC UNIX platforms have finally made these databases feasible for productive commercial applications.

Which Relational Database Is Right for You?

This question is actually weightier than it might appear at first because a database in the new environment is not just responsible for storing and retrieving data... it can also be responsible for much of the data's integrity and security for the distributed system. Some companies, in fact, are choosing to depend upon many of the functions, tools, and utilities of the more robust databases to ease the transition to the distributed environment. According to the MIS director of a major computer research company who recently downsized to a distributed platform of Oracle relational databases, "The Oracle database and tools shield most of the application programmers from having to know the underlying system. It automatically incorporates much of the commercial robustness required." Much of the functionality Oracle incorporates in its database products and tools is designed to compensate for the inherent difficulties of managing in the distributed environment. For instance, in its newest release V.7, Oracle has included automatic multiple site commit capability for simultaneous posting of incoming transactions to every database on the network...an important capability for companies who cannot afford to lose a transaction on their mission-critical systems. Other important relational database functions are: referential integrity (the ability to set data management and business rules when creating database tables), parallel server capability (for instantaneous cross-server filing), role-based security, and remote database administration.

The relational database world is not standing still. Vendors are leapfrogging each other in terms of functionality. Functionality not available from one vendor today is likely to be included in that vendor's next version. Thus, an assessment of a relational database vendor's longevity may be as important (if not more important) than scrutinizing today's features of its database products. The strongest relational database vendors in the U.S. market today are Oracle, INFORMIX, Sybase, Unify, and ASK/Ingres. The relative emphasis of these vendors has been: Oracle (larger- and mid-sized systems); INFORMIX (mid- to small-sized systems); Sybase (financial systems—close relationship with Dun & Bradstreet); Ingres (manufacturing—close relationship with ASK); and Unify (traditionally focused on smaller systems).

2. An Open Systems Server?

If the objective is simply to move to a distributed environment, it can be accomplished without moving to open systems. IBM mainframe users, for instance, can move to midrange AS/400 series midrange servers linked to IBM PCs using Novell LANs and SNA gateways. As discussed earlier, the distributed environment itself provides advantages that overcome many of the host/terminal issues. But why go through all the trouble to move to a new topology (involving software conversion, training the organization on new software packages, and building a new support structure) and still be hostage to one vendor's proprietary system?

Those familiar with UNIX, the flagship open systems operating system, are most likely also familiar with what many commercial users have viewed as insurmountable weaknesses of the UNIX operating system. UNIX was born in the free-wheeling researcher environment of AT&T's Bell Labs and was evolved by AT&T and numerous computer vendors into an effective compute-intensive operating system for engineers. The multi-tasking, multi-threaded capabilities of the UNIX operating system were extremely attractive to engineers who needed to continue to use their workstations even while they toiled away on lengthy calculations or time-consuming image processing. UNIX made it simple for the engineer to place the lengthy calculation in the background and continue with a separate activity in the foreground (such as developing a technical memo or running another calculation). Both operations were executed in parallel on the same CPU, and the engineer could switch at will between them. Since the operating system was designed by engineers and for engineers, very few of the safeguards necessary for protecting commercial computers against uninformed operator errors were incorporated...in fact, operator freedom was enhanced to the extreme. With UNIX, programs can be interrupted and placed at lower priority through "preemptive" instructions and even machine memory can be partitioned and used at will to allow an engineer to stuff extra code into the tiniest space.

The engineering world is also a world of global networks for open exchange of engineering ideas. The Internet, sponsored by the U.S. National Science Foundation, is one manifestation of this open exchange environment. It ties together millions of UNIX workstations on local- and wide-area networks around the world on a network powered by over 890,000 host machines and provides open access to news, electronic mail, electronic bulletin boards, and even "gopher" services for searching out phone numbers, computer documentation, weather, etc. Needless to say, in this environment, there is little interest in computer security. It should be no surprise therefore that the first commercial UNIX customers had trouble incorporating even the most rudimentary security measures into UNIX, for example, limiting access to sensitive data and applications by user group.

Little of what was carried out by researchers or engineers could be classified as "mission-critical" in the commercial sense of the term. If, for instance, an engineer inadvertently erased part of the computer's operating system through a mistake in his memory management commands and caused the system to crash, he may have lost some of his work and time; but his losses pale in comparison to the serious business losses a financial institution would incur, for instance, from data corruption or downtime on a country-wide automatic teller machine running at 100 to 1,000 transactions per second.

Many who checked out early UNIX versions on commercial applications went away believing that UNIX deficiencies in security and manageability were here for good. These deficiencies seemed to be a natural trade-off for the obvious advantages UNIX provided in engineering freedom.

Hardware platform vendors, however, did not give up on UNIX. Many saw the strong potential in UNIX for multiprocessing. The multiple threads of the UNIX operating system could be used for allocating processing jobs across numerous processing units in a server. As most vendors developed systems leveraging this and other unique UNIX capabilities, UNIX soon also became the only viable operating system candidate to be universally viewed as "multivendor" (and "open").

Many vendors formulated independent fixes for the UNIX operating system version that happened to be available at the time their particular development program started. This resulted in a world of multiple UNIX flavors. The major UNIX vendors, the UNIX kernels they employ, and their particular areas of emphasis are listed in Table 6-1.

The UNIX Wars (described in Chapter 1) created increased havoc in 1988, and informed the world just how fragmented UNIX really had become. Early versions of UNIX were weak with respect to commercial robustness. So what is the situation today?

Table 6-1: Varieties of UNIX

Vendor	Kernel Version	Special Focus
Hewlett-Packard	Sys V Rel 3	System Administration, Symmetric Multi-Processing(SMP)
Sun	Berkeley	SMP
IBM	Sys V Rel 3 enhanced to be compatible with BSD 4.3	Security
DEC	Sys V Rel 3.2	SMP
Apple A/UX	Sys V Rel 2.2 with some BSD 4.3 extensions	Multimedia
Open Software Foundation	Mach 2.5 Kernel	Commercial Features
Santa Cruz Operation	Sys V Rel 3.2	PC platform

Larry DeBoever of DeBoever Architectures claimed at a recent Downsizing Expo in San Francisco that commercial UNIX weaknesses are behind us. In his words, "Two years ago I would have advised you to stay on the mainframe because open systems were just not there when it came to commercial robustness...today I have changed my mind...things have changed....Now it is time to shoot the mainframe." Indeed, recent releases from UNIX Systems Labs (the UNIX development lab spun off from AT&T after the conclusion of the UNIX Wars) contain high-level security and multiprocessing capabilities incorporated in the UNIX kernel. USL's SVR4.1ES includes multiple methods of access control, trusted paths, and customizable audit trails. With these enhancements, UNIX is considered to have B2-level security, sufficient for many U.S. government programs. USL's SVR4MP release provides a multi-threaded kernel for concurrent operation of up to 16 processors, yet still retains an Application Binary Interface (ABI) compatibility with the straight SVR4 release. USL is predicting that they will merge these kernels to form a "Super UNIX" version with both the security and multiprocessing capabilities next year. The major U.S. hardware vendors are taking notice, and most are expected to release products offering compatibility with these newer kernel versions regardless of the side they took during the UNIX Wars.

But this is what the vendors and consultants are saying. Are there any UNIX customers who can testify to the maturing of UNIX...

especially regarding mission-critical applications, such as on-line transaction processing?

Putting Unix to the Test: GE Information Services

If any company is qualified to test UNIX in the toughest commercial environments, it is probably GE Information Services (GEIS). The types of applications they run for their customers range from financial risk management, through custom systems for some of the world's major corporations, to a range of electronic commerce services. They are the largest suppliers of electronic data interchange services in the U.S., and are a major player in the field of electronic mail and on-line information services. To run these services, GEIS operates computer services in the U.S. and Europe. The largest of these is a 2.5-acre site packed with mainframe clusters running 7 days a week, 24 hours a day. The GEIS team has built much of the software, including a multiprocessing operating system, and CPU and data switchover clustering utilities, that combined with other tools and technologies, enables them to run their centers with minimal operations staffs.

According to Roger Dyer, Manager of Platform Engineering, GEIS's missions have been to run operations their customers (1) could not run themselves, due to technology, economies of scale, or the global reach GEIS offers; or (2) do not want to manage themselves. A typical #2 mission would be, for instance, an EDI operation for the retail industry. Such an operation requires many companies, who might naturally be competitors, to interchange orders and shipping information. GEIS, as the service supplier, can ensure that security is maintained by acting as the neutral third party, and at the same time assuring that each participant in the EDI "network" receives their orders and reports...and only their orders and reports. Whether the mission is #1 or #2, much of their business is related to the flow of commerce and funds... the type of applications placing the toughest demands on system reliability, data integrity, security, and manageability. This does not sound like a place to see UNIX, right? But look again! GEIS is running mission-critical applications on UNIX servers today, and more are planned. In fact, they have a major development effort underway to build their next generation electronic commerce services on UNIX.

The first mission-critical GEIS UNIX operation was installed in response to a customer request for an open systems-based solution for a new version of an existing application. It is an insurance claims processing application, which originally ran on an IBM mainframe, and now runs on a triplet of midsize HP-UX servers. These systems provide switch-over and data-pair capabilities that meet GEIS's stringent reliability and availability requirements. They also have other UNIX applications running today: one for petroleum price notifications to brokers, and another for X.500 directory services. GEIS has more applications in the pipeline, including migrating their mainframe-based X.400 services. By 1997, Mr. Dyer expects to see a "large percentage of GEIS's applications on UNIX."

GEIS's move to open systems was not sparked by high dissatisfaction with proprietary mainframe systems. Mr. Dyer will tell you that proprietary systems have provided GEIS with many important advantages including, "total control of the hardware and software operating environment plus high availability and reliability, all adding up to top notch quality standards." His reasons for moving over to UNIX are compelling. "If the hardware vendors fails you or their equipment costs too much, you can change vendors," he observes. "That is the driving force in the open systems market...it is the force that squeezes vendors to reduce costs with the newest technologies. The open systems market is delivering a world where the cost of MIPS is close to nothing and memory is also cheap." He goes on to point out that open systems can also be highly scalable. "Our mainframe technology comes in one size—large—whereas we can scale an open system to the local demand. We can start out small and expand capacity as time goes on, by upgrades or adding more systems. Since, within a family, the systems are compatible, no software rewrites are necessary."

GEIS had been looking at UNIX and microprocessor-based systems since the mid-80s, so they had experience watching UNIX develop before deciding to start a UNIX program in 1989. What they found was that UNIX had come a long way in functionality and manageability. In Mr. Dyer's opinion, "Everything worked." He has, however, highlighted the weaker areas and has worked with UNIX platform vendors to improve them. One concern is the lack of sufficient "fire walls" between applications on the same CPU. "On the UNIX platform, a misbehaving or runaway application can cause too much impact to other applications. Our mainframes still do a better job of separating out the jobs and resources." At GEIS, where the business is running many thousands of sessions simultaneously, this is a significant drawback. Another area of concern is software resilience. Mainframe loads are very volatile, and jumps of 1,000 plus on-line users in very short timeframes are not unusual.

For the time being, GEIS runs their UNIX servers at 50-75% capacity levels "just in case." Even at this loading, they are very pleased with the operating cost equation, which is significantly better than the mainframe world.

When asked what his advice to Japanese MIS directors working in the mainframe environment might be, Mr. Dyer replied, "If I were in a Japanese company with a more controlled computing environment than GEIS (less fluctuation in loads, fewer fire walls required, etc.), I would not hesitate to go flat out and downsize to UNIX... because in that environment, you should easily see five-to-one savings."

GEIS and many of the other companies cited in this book are downsizing to UNIX. Does that mean UNIX is appropriate for everyone? Perhaps, but there are still many companies purchasing proprietary systems, even as they downsize. What are their reasons, and how do those reasons stand up?

Most U.S. companies choosing to go with proprietary systems in their downsizing strategies are trying to reduce costs without greatly disrupting their MIS environments. Although shifting a financial application from an IBM 4381 system to an IBM AS/400 may require extra programming and some new system management schemes, the supporting vendor is still the same old familiar IBM. Since IBM is already aware of the company's needs, some MIS managers expect that the proprietary downsized solution is more likely to meet those needs. Moreover, if IBM has provided strong support and service in the past, that level of support and service is likely to continue. Introducing a new vendor into the environment brings in uncertainties not only with respect to the new technology, but also with respect to troubleshooting computer problems. The last thing an MIS director wants is two vendors pointing fingers at each other when the system goes down.

This argument would be compelling if we were not in an age marked by discontinuous change. Today, no single vendor can continue to provide leading edge components for all parts of an enterprise-wide system. There is already a clear difference in price between open and proprietary systems. Already, the software community is moving its best applications onto the leading price performance RISC/UNIX platforms. The price curves are declining at greater than 60-70% per year today, and there is every indication that the curve will get steeper, not flatter. Can you trust your proprietary vendor to keep up? What if a strong competitor in your industry is able to use the superior price performance of open systems to squeeze more competitive advantage out of their MIS system than you? Will your customers know the difference? Do you want to take that chance?

Should you start learning UNIX after your competitor makes the move? MIS directors interviewed for this book think not. Most of them believe that MIS directors need to move now so they can remain in control of evolving their systems. Remaining in control means being able to accurately assess the merits of each new open systems package, tool, or utility...and accurate assessment requires familiarity with open system operations. To many MIS directors, this familiarity is becoming a basic requirement for running a successful MIS shop.

3. What Type of Client?

The options for desktop clients expand every few months as lower cost and enhanced functionality devices hit the market at a dizzying pace. Here are just a few generic choices available today for consideration:

Desktop PCs: PCs are by far the most popular device for the desktop. For many, the decision to move to PCs has already been made by user groups in the company who have taken the initiative to purchase PCs for word processing and spreadsheet analysis on a stand-alone basis, or connected through local area networks (most often Netware from Novell). These users typically purchased their PCs to obtain:

- Local processing power to create memos or do analysis when they want to, and in the way they want to

- Local printing

- Local filing to get paper out of their files but not so far away that it is inconvenient, for instance, locked up in a mainframe

- Access to data to obtain financial information, news briefs, and other information from the countless data services available through a dial-up PC modem

Laptop PCs: Same as desktop PCs, but laptop users purchase with the additional objective of being able to do word processing, spreadsheet calculations, etc., no matter where they find themselves. Sales representatives use them to check product inventory on the road and process customer billings on-site.

Some users simply want to conserve space on the desktop. Customers have to pay more for these conveniences. The price per MIP of a laptop is generally higher than that for a desktop PC.

UNIX Workstations: As mentioned above, UNIX workstations are usually found in engineering and software development environments, and are chosen for computing power, multi-tasking flexibility, or UNIX-based development tools, such as 4GLs. UNIX workstation capabilities are also becoming attractive to commercial desktop "power" users, whose jobs are computation-intensive or require much work group interaction.

X-Terminals: X-terminals provide an inexpensive alternative to UNIX workstations for placing a graphical user interface on the desktop. The MIPS of a powerful server can be efficiently shared by multiple X-terminals. The terminals include a separate graphics subsystem for generating the graphical user interface, yet depend upon a server for running the operating system, application software, and networking. X-terminals are also relatively easy to manage. Application upgrades, for instance, only need to be installed at the server to change over the whole work group. X-server software is also becoming available on PCs, but considerable power is necessary to operate the interface.

All of the above desktop options come in diskless versions for companies looking to simplify software management and enhance security. Fewer floppy disks entering the system means less chance of contracting an intractable computer virus.

Terminals: Dumb terminals can be left in place and operated using multi-user terminal connect software or the IBM 3270 emulation software normally used for linking into IBM mainframe systems. This is by far the least expensive desktop device available, especially if it is already installed for communicating with the mainframe. Since these terminals do not have the intelligence to provide a graphical user interface, support user task logic (such as input error checking and editing), or run any local applications, few advantages of distributed computing can be realized. The data storage and compute burden of the client is placed 100% on the servers. Since every keystroke by a user needs to be interpreted by the server, the traffic on the network can easily become excessive.

Again, which desktop device to choose? Companies today are generally choosing PCs with graphical user interfaces (such as Windows from Microsoft) for the desktop, and for sales and marketing rep applications, laptops are often preferred. For the software development and engineering environments, you guessed it, UNIX workstations and X-terminals are the choices. UNIX workstations, however, are also finding their way into the commercial side of the business. As mentioned earlier, many companies are using them for analyzing decision support data in large spreadsheets at the headquarters or regional offices. Dealing rooms at securities firms and banking operations are also opening their doors to UNIX desktop devices. The compute-intensity of such operations lend themselves to powerful RISC/UNIX multi-tasking machines. UNIX desktop machines are coming down in price sufficiently to compete with their PC brethren, which run on the more traditional CISC Intel chips. When making your desktop decisions, it makes sense to keep testing the UNIX desktop waters to see whether the price performance and software available in the UNIX market can provide sufficient value to justify installation of UNIX on the desktops of your company. Having a system that totally runs on UNIX allows for common protocols and system management tools, making overall system management much simpler.

4. How to Tie It All Together?

Getting the network right is one of the most important elements for achieving success with downsizing. Those who have gone through a major downsizing experience generally emphasize four points:

- Standardize
- Install extra bandwidth
- Replace bridges
- Provide sufficient networking support

Standardize: Networks and desktop applications/operating systems must be standardized or bugs will be nearly impossible to diagnose correctly in a downsized client/server environment. Larry DeBoever, of DeBoever Architectures, believes in insisting that users not only use the same application packages, but also the same version of application package. This is especially important for conducting software upgrades centrally from a system management server.

Local area networks should also be standardized. Both token ring and Ethernet LANs work fine in most environments and network configurations can be adjusted to run the LANs at traffic volumes most appropriate for the chosen LAN protocol. The point is, rather than choosing the right LAN, it is more important to choose just one type of LAN and stick with it throughout the system. It is certainly not impossible to link heterogeneous LANs together with multiprotocol routers and bridges, but that adds an unnecessary layer of complexity to an already complex system topology.

Another important set of decisions revolve around the desktop and LAN operating systems. Novell's netware is the current market leader in PC LAN operating systems with close to 70% share. Recent moves by Novell and UNIX Systems Labs (USL) to introduce a UNIX/Netware hybrid, Univel, helps bring the worlds of Netware, UNIX, and TCP/IP even closer together, making a Netware choice even more appropriate as a downsizing LAN OS for the time being. For desktop operating systems today, the two major contenders as of this publishing are Microsoft Windows on DOS and IBM's OS/2. Over ten million copies of Windows have been sold vs. a very respectable one million copies for late starter OS/2. Recent user assessments are pointing to OS/2 as the more stable environment, and so OS/2 may continue to grow at Windows' expense.

Unfortunately, the battle over the desktop operating system and LAN OS market is too volatile today to predict any sure future winners beyond 1992. As mentioned in Chapter 1, numerous companies with substantial market influence are focusing their resources on this part of the market. The jury is still out on whether Microsoft's highly publicized Windows NT object-oriented desktop operating system—boasting multi-threading, multiprocessor support, security, portability, client/server networking, and basic fault tolerance—will sweep the market after its introduction in July 1993. IBM and Apple have joined together in a joint venture to create a company called Taligent, chartered to develop another object-oriented operating system to leapfrog Windows NT (or the next-generation NT, incorporating Microsoft's object technology from its CAIRO project). Sun Microsystems is providing ISVs with development versions of a low-end "Solaris 2.0" UNIX operating system for an Intel desktop platform. The Univel challenger was mentioned above, and even Steve Jobs, the famous founder of Apple Computer, is joining the fray with his Next Step operating system, which, as usual for Mr. Jobs, contains technical features surpassing all other systems.

My advice would be to buy either Windows or OS/2 on UNIX today, and take a wait-and-see perspective on the newer object-oriented systems. We are talking about a major shift in technologies with objects, and so the initial versions can be expected to be delayed, or introduced with bugs. Moreover, many of the companies will need to develop stronger distribution and support channels before achieving market-wide acceptance for their products. Many have pushed their past products through low-value-added dealers, so moving up to distributing more complex object-oriented products may be a significant challenge.

Install Extra Bandwidth: Err on the side of putting in place extra network bandwidth because it is bound to come in handy as traffic climbs with more user access to the system. Larry DeBoever cites the results of a recent AT&T experiment for future wide area networking service to illustrate that not only MIPS, but networking is also becoming "free." AT&T apparently raised the data transmit speed on a 9,800-mile circuit to 10 gigabits per second for a full hour and recorded zero errors. Mr. DeBoever goes on to say that with a networking link like that, a host could boot a PC 3,000 miles away virtually as fast as the PC could be booted off a local server. Ten gigabits per second is faster than the internal bus of even the quickest computers.

Even though this type of super speed networking is not available today, faster wide area networking is in the offing. It may make sense while you have the construction crew laying your cable, to put in enough bandwidth to ensure your backbone does not become next year's bottleneck. Mr. DeBoever suggests a data grade 5 UTP (Unshielded Twisted Pair) since it will support 100-megabit Ethernet networks at a cost that is only 10-15% greater than DG 4 UTP, which is used in most 10-megabit Ethernets.

Another reason for installing extra bandwidth is the difficulty in accurately predicting traffic volumes for the new environment. Users who have been fettered by bottlenecks on the mainframe and uncooperative user interfaces are liberated under the new system and often become ravenous for data and applications, boosting traffic on the network by several orders of magnitude. Mystified by this phenomenon, Mr. DeBoever once asked users whether they would download all of the data in their corporate database to their PC if they could do it in 15 minutes. As he suspected, many responded in the affirmative.

Replace the Bridges: With the increased traffic comes a need for better traffic control around the network. One important first step taken by many downsizing companies is to rip out all of the bridges and replace them with more intelligent routers. Bridges, for the most part, act only as filters (filtering out messages addressed to remote systems for passage across the bridge) and simple protocol translators, performing such functions as Ethernet-to-token ring LAN conversion. Routers, by comparison, not only filter, but also direct traffic from LAN to LAN, adding enhanced networking efficiency and manageability.

Systems from a variety of vendors are often connected in the downsized system, requiring complex protocol conversions, for instance, TCP/IP (generally regarded as the open systems networking protocol) to IBM's SNA, or Digital Equipment Corporation's DECnet. For this type of conversion, gateways, or the more sophisticated routers, are required.

The system management benefits of routers also come in handy. Some provide remote protocol update capabilities and access through a separate line for out-of-band diagnosis and control. This is especially handy when trouble spots around a router are too congested to access through the normal channels.

Routers may be more expensive than bridges, but the downtime and debugging problems avoided by switching to routers early on in the process easily pay for the difference in price.

Provide Sufficient Network Support: Marc Dodge, MIS director at United Parcel Service (UPS), stated in a recent talk at the San Francisco Downsizing Expo that he firmly believes that strong networking support saved the day for his MIS staff during their downsizing program at UPS, which took them from their first LAN in 1987 to over 1,000 in 1992. The downsized applications include such innovative systems as LAN-attached delivery clipboards for collecting shipping information and passing it automatically to mainframe databases for permanent storage. 60,000 of these devices are now in use every day by UPS drivers around the U.S. Another is a customer service network for tracking packages, so customer questions on the whereabouts of a specific package can be answered immediately over the telephone whatever the origin or destination. Mr. Dodge has a slide of how the tracking office looked before the system was put into operation. Not surprisingly, paper was piled from floor to ceiling, and operators were searching the shelves for package information. That image contrasts sharply with the nearly paperless office they operate today.

Mr. Dodge's IS organization also grew proportionately during the program from 125 employees to 3,000 in 1992 (1,200 in the New Jersey headquarters and 1,800 spread out around the country). Divide the 1,800 staff members located outside headquarters by the 1,000 LANs, and the ratio is 1.8 IS members per LAN around UPS' geographically dispersed network. Mr. Dodge believes the correct ratio for network support is 1 support person for every 100 LAN users.

His reasons for planting support person power around his network, however, extends beyond calculations of LAN downtime and system efficiencies. He will tell you they are necessary, to gain the trust of the user community, especially during the uneasy time of transition. "It gives the users the impression that MIS has their interests at heart," he said. "Once users view MIS in a positive light, they support MIS even when the inevitable mistakes are made during the transition program."

Mr. Dodge is convinced that extra support is also necessary because "it is human nature that all problems in the system get blamed on the last thing that has been changed." During a major transition program, the last thing that was changed generally has something to do with MIS, so calls for all types of problems come to Mr. Dodge's staff. To address this natural user tendency effectively, he has spent time training MIS support staff to bend over backwards in resolving user concerns avoiding potential "bad raps." User calls are to be followed up on until fully resolved...and being "resolved," in his organization, means that the user agrees that the problem is fixed.

Most LAN roll-outs will not require quite the magnitude of LANs and support staff as that for UPS' geographically dispersed network of delivery offices, but Mr. Dodge's advice on the importance of user support is relevant for technology programs in general, and especially those involving client/server implementations. As mentioned in Chapter 3, Wayne Pendleton, American Airline's Managing Director of Advanced Office Systems, met with significant user resistance to his initial client/server roll-out. He responded by changing the mission of his staff from "technology provision" to "joint information technology partnering." Mr. Pendleton, however, did not use the human wave approach employed at UPS. Rather than assigning remote IS staff to each LAN, he avoided excessive expansion of MIS support staff by leveraging resources within the user divisions. As mentioned earlier, IT facilitators were assigned in each user group to take on the non-technical system work, and IS training was made mandatory for all operators on the American Airlines system.

5. How to Manage the Network?

Managing the downsized system is probably one of the greatest concerns of any downsizing shop. With the distributed system, not only is computing power spread out over countless locations and geographies, the software is also dispersed. Moreover, the system is like a patchwork quilt of differing vendor machines, operating systems, protocols, and networking links. Downsizing may dramatically lower IS cost and bring information closer to the users, but at the same time, it increases the complexity of the MIS system management job by several orders of magnitude.

Some companies have gone out of their way to reduce the distributed management burden by placing all of their new RISC/UNIX servers in one place, say, the old glass house. Although moving from glass house mainframes to glass house servers helps by shifting applications to less expensive MIPS, it is not usually effective for companies with geographically dispersed locations. Data transmission is slowed considerably by high dependence on slower WAN lines (although this may change in the more distant future if AT&T's 10-gigabit experiment produces fruit).

For most companies, however, distributed computing is truly distributed and the above set of complexities quickly become serious system management challenges. Are there tools on the market today that make managing the new system as easy as managing a mainframe central topology? As Bill Williams from Liteline remarked, "Once you take a look at SNMP and OpenView, you will find most of it there... and what is not there on day one will be here soon." SNMP (Simple Network Management Protocol) is the industry-standard networking management protocol adhered to by most networking and platform vendors. Vendor devices adhering to SNMP transmit system management messages in standard SNMP language across the network to enable management servers to monitor such things as the address, configuration, and operating status of each device. SNMP itself is not sufficient for conducting many essential system management tasks, such as fault, configuration, performance, and security management. These functions are provided by system management software packages from a variety of vendors. HP's OpenView is the system management utility with the largest share position today (according to a 1992 survey by International Data Corp). OpenView's aim is to allow managers in the "glass house" to monitor most systems, including IBM, Sun, and HP UNIX devices, on the TCP/IP network. It provides them with the ability to know how the devices are configured, whether they are operational or not, and whether performance is up to expectation. OpenView also guards against security breaches through object level authorization with audit trails. Any more questions? I am sure there are.

How about other vendor system management products? The second largest market share position is held by Sun's SunNet Manager, which also offers much of what is delivered by OpenView. One area of relative weakness in the Sun software is "node discovery." A recent article in *Open Systems Today*[1] describes OpenView's Network Node Manager as "capable of automatically discovering all nodes on the interconnected LANs and even checking for illegal addresses and incorrect submasks. OpenView then displays nodes and connections on a network map, and updates the network map when logical changes occur." The article's assessment of the SunNet manager capabilities in this area was not as positive: "SunNet seeks IP and SNMP addressable devices, creating a network map that depicts the devices in default configuration. However, this means that actual connections between nodes or subnets are not automatically displayed. The user must draw these in. And changes to the network are not automatically detected." OpenView also obtains higher marks with respect to uploading vendor-specific information contained in MIB (Management Information Base) packets...packets which are especially helpful in managing non-standard devices and features.

Other vendors, for instance NetLabs and Cabletron Spectrum, also provide similar system management tools. These tools are weaker in the above mentioned "node discovery" area but have strengths in such functions as alarm/event filtering. OpenView and SunNet are likely to continue outselling these other products, because their already acquired larger market presence is leading to expanded third-party development on their platforms. Active third-party development leads to greater connectivity with the multitude of system components sold in the market, and in turn, greater market acceptance. for instance, third-party efforts provided HP's OpenView with connectivity to IBM/SNA and PC/Netware, extra security features, and 4GL tools. According to the same *Open Systems Today* article mentioned above, "HP has won praise because it establishes

---

1. Dewar, Robert B.K., and Smosna, Matthew, "Making Heterogeneous Nets Hum," *Open Systems Today,* Sep.14, 1992, 44–46.

different levels of partnership, and encourages and rewards vendors that make commitments to the HP OpenView platform." HP should have little trouble maintaining a lead in the number of high-quality system management partners. OpenView technology was virtually accepted "as-is" for incorporation in OSF's Distributed Management Environment (DME) open bidding and selection process.

Another option, popular among mainframe users of Computer Associate's CA-UNICENTER suite of mainframe system management tools, is to use Computer Associates' version of these tools for UNIX. The UNICENTER console management, workload management, spooled print controls, report distribution control, automated storage management, security control, problem tracking, performance monitoring, and resource accounting are all there in the UNIX version, according to Computer Associates.

How about transaction monitoring? Transaction monitoring, the software environment for on-line transaction processing, protects transaction integrity through cross-system database and utility updating during a transaction, "all-or-nothing" rules that return the system to the last stable status in the event of incomplete transactions, and numerous other system availability and data security features. Is there an equivalent in the distributed computing environment?

Customers who have grown to depend on IBM's CICS (Customer Information and Control System) or another transaction monitor environment may have been relieved to read in Chapter 5 that CICS is being ported to UNIX. IBM has already announced CICS versions for their AIX RS6000 line and for HP's HP-UX platform. CICS on UNIX servers allows downsizing MIS departments to continue to leverage their CICS development skills (acquired over the years with IBM mainframes) even in the new environment. A recent article in *Open Systems Today* (September 14,1992) quotes an MIS manager excited about the prospect of CICS on UNIX, "CICS may or may not be the best from a technological point of view, but we have a huge investment in mainframe CICS, and we look at this as a way to leverage our training, staff skills and existing software investment....There's some possibility in the future that we may want a non-CICS transaction monitor, but to launch us from mainframes to smaller machines, this is the way to go."

Other transaction processing monitors developed, or being developed, for the distributed environment are likely to contain important distributed environment advantages and also to carry less baggage from the mainframe environment. These may be of special interest to MIS departments with less of a CICS history. The two major contenders are: Encina (Transarc), a transaction processing environment built on many of the standard OSF modules included in OSF's Distributed Computing Environment (DCE), and Tuxedo (by USL), introduced initially in July, 1991 for the UNIX international camp of the UNIX Wars. Encina is expected to become available on HP, Stratus, SunOS, NEC and Hitachi. Tuxedo is available on HP, DEC, Sun, SCO, Sequent, Tandem, Unisys and 17 other companies' systems.

How about high availability? Companies with time-urgent applications know the importance of high availability and realize the cost difference between running a 99.5% availability system vs. 99.8%. Figure 6-1 shows the calculated difference in annual costs for running a range of systems from 99.5% availability to 99.995%.

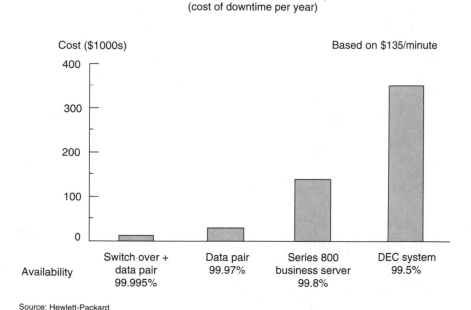

Figure 6-1: *Annual downtime costs.*

Assuming business costs are $135 per minute downtime, the 99.995% availability system can save a company over $300,000 per year.

The value of higher-availability systems is, of course, greater for companies with more urgent business applications. If occasional downtime incidents of one to two hours do not cause problems in the running of your business, a basic platform with 99.5% or 99.8% availability is probably sufficient. The less expensive option in this range today exists with the HP-UX platforms, which provide 99.8% availability. These systems have an MBTF (Mean Time Between Failures) of four years. If a company's operations include on-line transaction processing, however, higher availability options should also be considered.

The next higher level of availability is attainable through disk mirroring with data disk pairs. Duplicate disks are created using disk mirroring to avoid information loss and minimize system downtime in the event of a disk failure. Disk mirroring also reduces the need for "planned downtime" for backing up the system. On-line system backup can be done from the second disk using utilities, such as HP's OmniBack and OmniBack Turbo. The same data protection can also be provided at lower cost by using RAID technology (Redundant Array of Inexpensive Disks), which minimizes the number of backup disks. With RAID, various techniques are used (usually bit and block interleaving) so that four disks can be backed up by one "parity" disk.

The next option for increasing availability, in HP's case from 99.97% to 99.995%, is system switchover. As the name implies, system switchover provides automatic recovery in the event of system failure. A standby server running non-mission-critical applications is used as a switchover backup system. The standby system takes over within 10 to 25 minutes if a mission-critical application server fails.

Fully redundant fault-tolerant systems provide the highest levels of availability achievable today. These systems provide uninterrupted operation with an average recovery time of less than ten seconds. No data reaching main memory is ever lost. System vendors with fault tolerant systems include HP, Sequoia, and Stratus. Some high-availability solutions are available from DEC (on VAX proprietary), IBM and Sun (disk mirroring), and Sequent (CPU backup and disk mirroring). HP and Pyramid provide a complete set of high-availability offerings on their systems.

6. Which Hardware Vendor to Choose?

Choosing the hardware vendor can be one of the most difficult decisions in a downsizing effort. Since I work for HP, I certainly do not qualify as an unbiased guide to resolving this question. Nevertheless, I am lucky to be working at a vendor I can strongly recommend without misgivings.

Let me quickly sketch out where I see other vendors going with their strategies and then explain why HP is the most appropriate choice for the vast majority of companies embarking on downsizing today.

IBM has continued to exhibit a strong bias toward keeping its customers on the mainframe platform...and for those who insist on moving to smaller systems, they have directed them to the AS/400 proprietary platform in lieu of their AIX (UNIX) RS6000 series. The proprietary platform locks in customers to buying IBM systems and components in the future, and most likely provides IBM with higher margins. The recent announcements of IBM losses, the shedding of personnel through severance incentive programs, and the reorganization of IBM into separate businesses, however, has substantially changed IBM as a company. More recently, IBM is reportedly becoming more aggressive in selling their RS6000 line.

Perhaps due to IBM's prior lack of emphasis on UNIX, the AIX operating system has been plagued with bugs which, according to some users, have still not been completely worked out. As mentioned above, IBM's high-availability offerings on the RS6000 line are limited as well. The IBM plan is to close the gap between their UNIX offerings and competing vendors during 1993–94. They expect to be able to deliver simultaneous multiprocessing capabilities (through their recently consummated relationship with Bull in France), enhanced UNIX kernel threads, most of OSF's Distributed Computing Environment (DCE) functionality, and cluster/high-availability enhancements in IBM's next set of AIX releases.

As mentioned above, IBM's software organization (which is also driven by a more independent strategy since the IBM reorganization) is porting IBM's CICS transaction processing environment to their AIX platform, as well as to other computing platforms (such as HP). One stop-gap measure IBM is employing to keep customers on IBM systems, is the leveraging of non-IBM system software. IBM's high opinion of HP's software is evidenced by their decision to license HP's Softbench CASE tool environment and OpenView for their AIX systems.

In short, IBM is playing catch-up in the open systems market. This is also true with respect to their hardware system performance. IBM's most recent release lags the industry leader in price/performance (HP) by a full $4,000 per transaction per second (see Figure 6-2) according to recent benchmarkings conducted using INFORMIX 4.0 relational database software. The benchmarking was done by an industry-wide recognized performance council, using a well-regarded TPC-A benchmarking measure.

Sun Microsystems' early success in the engineering workstation market has given them a broad base of engineering customers and substantial volumes to leverage into the commercial market. Some of

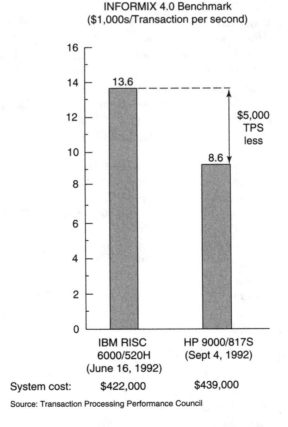

Figure 6-2: HP vs. IBM: price performance.

Sun's technologies, such as Sun's Network File System (NFS), have become standard fixtures in UNIX systems from all vendors. More recently, serious weaknesses in Sun's underlying SPARC chip architecture have left Sun behind in price performance as HP delivered significantly superior single chip performance. This has led Sun to introduce multiprocessing at performance levels easily managed by HP's more powerful single processor systems. Few users prefer multiprocessing over single processing if the performance is the same. Extra CPUs tend to introduce additional complexity, and complexity often undermines reliability. Sun is overcoming this weakness through development of "SuperSparc" systems based on a revised chip architecture, but the change is costing valuable time and placing limitations on new operating system development, to which they need to provide a smooth migration path for their current users.

The Sun management team has also shown a keen interest in charting their own independent UNIX path. Their confidence in this area has probably stemmed from Sun's history of holding the leading market share position in engineering workstations. Sun's close ties with AT&T in 1987 led other vendors to believe Sun would get an unfair advantage in setting the direction for UNIX. As mentioned in Chapter 1, this led to the establishment of a rival UNIX organization, OSF—backed by IBM, HP, and DEC—and the start of the UNIX wars. Even after the UNIX wars subsided, Sun continued to chart a separate course. Long after OSF's "Motif" was accepted as the industry standard graphical interface, Sun held fast to its homegrown interface, "OpenLook." Only after much pressure was applied by Sun users operating in mixed environments, did Sun agree to also support Motif. Over the last year, Sun has become more cooperative, according to David Tory of OSF. He was quoted in *Open Systems Today* (September 28, 1992) as saying that OSF and Sun have been working together to integrate OSF's DCE and DME technologies with Sun's networking technologies. To what extent Sun has turned over a new leaf, however, has been recently brought into question by the finding that Sun quietly provided $7.5 million of backing to fund a lawsuit against OSF by a third-party ISV, Addamax. The Addamax case is apparently a "sour grapes" complaint against OSF for not choosing Addamax's security tools in the open bidding OSF process. Sun's attempts to take UNIX independent are viewed by many as counter-productive to the UNIX open systems cause, because there is little difference between an independent UNIX and a proprietary system.

Sun's history as an engineering workstation vendor weakens its candidacy as a hardware vendor for downsizing companies in other ways as well. The mainframe vendors and minicomputer vendors (HP and DEC) have all acquired knowledge about the special needs of companies running mission-critical commercial applications through many years of selling solutions into the commercial environment. Michael Bauer of EDS articulates the difference between engineering and commercial worlds with the following example: "An engineer may get excited about a hot box that can grind out calculations faster, but a payroll manager may be scared to death by the same box. The box may churn out payroll a few hours faster, but without the system software infrastructure to ensure it will work every time...there may be days when the system goes down and payroll is delayed not only for a few hours, but by a day or so. This type of uncertainty is not permissible at most companies because a delay in payroll can reflect badly on the company image to its employees, stockholders, and ultimately, its customers."

A company without extensive history in delivering robust commercial systems often needs to depend excessively on outside vendors to provide the core functionality. Sun is working closely with two companies in particular, Tivoli and Transarc, to incorporate as many functions from OSF's DCE into its own operating system.

Sun is also aiming to play a major role on the desktop with its low-end version of the Solaris operating system, Solaris 2.0, designed for Intel PC platforms. The jury is still out on desktop operating systems, as I mentioned earlier, but ISVs have shown only limited interest so far in the low-end Solaris system.

In summation, Sun's aggressive bid to control the UNIX world has been undermined by the combined strengths of other computer vendors, and by limitations in their own RISC technology. Sun is now aiming to take the lead in defining the desktop and also is attempting, through close relationships with third parties, to establish a foothold in the larger system commercial marketplace.

Available benchmarking comparisons for Sun using Oracle V.7 (see Figure 6-3) show a relative weakness of roughly $2,000 per TPS, according to the Transaction Processing Performance Council.

Digital Equipment Corporation (DEC) found its price performance sputtering late in 1991. DEC also found its plans to depend on the ACE consortium for underlying chip technology heading toward trouble as MIPS, the primary chip developing company for ACE, floundered in red ink. The ACE consortium has unraveled since then and DEC is betting on three areas for the future:

1. DEC has developed a powerful 64-bit chip architecture called Alpha for which the first implementations shipped at the end of 1992.

2. DEC is trying to build widespread acceptance of its Network Architecture System (NAS) platform (containing network administration and operation system software utilities and tools) through such activities as porting to competitor platforms, etc.

3. DEC has made an early commitment to shipping Microsoft's anxiously awaited Windows NT next-generation desktop and networking operating system product on its Alpha platform,

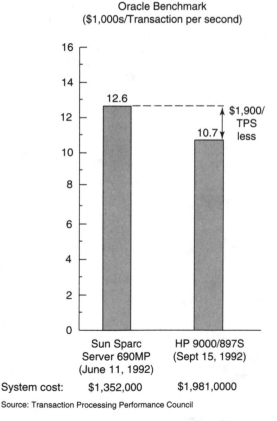

Figure 6-3: HP vs. Sun: price performance.

and is hedging bets by shipping the OSF/1 operating system on DEC's MIPs platform as well. DEC claims these two systems are compatible.

DEC, like the other vendors mentioned so far, is playing catch-up on a few fronts. First of all DEC's new president, Robert Palmer, is fighting to cut costs to overcome massive losses incurred this year. Mr. Palmer plans to let go 25,000 to 30,000 employees, according to an October 1992 *PC Week* article.[2] Secondly, DEC has had a meandering strategy with respect to open systems because of an apparent personal bias against UNIX by the prior president and founder of the 33-year-old computer vendor, Ken Olsen, who resigned in July of 1992. This bias led DEC to underinvest in its UNIX programs. Limitations in its high-availability offerings on its UNIX platform called ULTRIX (previously mentioned) is symptomatic of the low-priority status ULTRIX development engineers struggled with at DEC. It may make sense to wait until DEC puts its financial house in order and sets a clear platform direction before considering DEC for a central role in your downsizing program.

Available benchmarks for DEC use INFORMIX 4.1, so comparisons are more difficult. Nevertheless, a comparison to HP running INFORMIX 4.0 reveals a large $9,400 gap in TPS (see Figure 6-4). DEC is trying to overcome this poor showing, as previously mentioned, with its newly developed "Alpha" RISC chips.

Sequent Computer Systems Inc. is an Oregon-based system platform start-up (first product sold in December 1984) that sells symmetrical multiprocessing computers, mostly for dedicated On-Line Transaction Processing (OLTP) applications. Sequent's systems incorporate arrays of inexpensive Intel PC chips managed by proprietary system software to provide superior price performance in the pure OLTP environment, i.e., where individual transactions are simple, but flowing in high volumes. Sequent's OLTP strengths catapulted the company from $20 million in 1986 revenues to greater than $213 million in 1991.

Sequent's machines, however, have serious drawbacks when it comes to batch processing. Since batch processes are single threaded, they need to be executed on a single CPU. On the Sequent platform, the single CPU is inevitably an Intel chip (typically used for PCs). Clearly, it does not make sense to run an important batch pro-

---

2. Musich, Paula, and Burke, Steven, "Palmer's Plan Calls for Leaner DEC," *PC Week,* Oct. 5, 1992, 1,12.

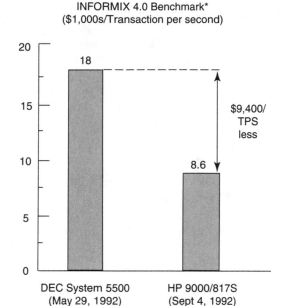

INFORMIX 4.0 Benchmark*
($1,000s/Transaction per second)

System cost: $379,000 $439,0000

* The DEC benchmark uses Informix 4.1. INFORMIX 4.0 benchmark results were not available
for DEC at time of publication.

Source: Transaction Processing Performance Council

Figure 6-4: *HP vs. DEC: price performance.*

cess, such as payroll for a sizable company, on the equivalent of a
PC. Since most companies have needs both in the OLTP and batch
environment, they go to other vendors for general-purpose servers
that incorporate more powerful single processors and can handle
both these activities without a hitch.

During 1990, Sequent's profits started heading south, and in
1991, Sequent recorded a $49 million deficit. The Sequent manage-
ment team is now in the process of restructuring the company to
hoist it back to a level of sustainable profitability.

For companies interested in a point OLTP platform, Sequent
may be appropriate to consider. Sequent's financial problems, however, may undermine its ability to make the necessary investments
to keep up with the price performance and other capabilities of more
stable competitor platforms. Already, general-purpose servers from
HP show both superior OLTP price performance to Sequent (on well-
regarded benchmarks) and much quicker batch processing on a sin-

gle platform. Whatever the application, it may be prudent to check out other more general-purpose server options thoroughly before settling on Sequent as your major hardware platform vendor.

Sequent trails HP by $4,700 per TPC on INFORMIX 4.0 benchmarks, according to the Transaction Processing Performance Council (Figure 6-5).

Japanese Vendors: Commercial UNIX is a relative newcomer to Japan. Few, if any, contributions to UNIX technology have been made by Japanese vendors. For the most part, Japanese vendors have been monitoring the progress of open systems from the sidelines. Their participation has been limited to joining both sides during the UNIX Wars, OEMing U.S. UNIX workstation platforms to sell into both engineering and commercial markets in Japan, and introducing UNIX as an "extra" feature on some of their midrange systems.

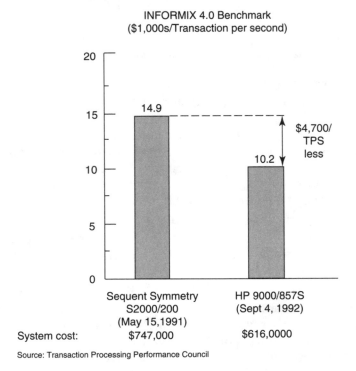

INFORMIX 4.0 Benchmark
($1,000s/Transaction per second)

Source: Transaction Processing Performance Council

Figure 6-5: *HP vs. Sequent: price performance.*

Since most Japanese vendors plan to continue to sell UNIX platforms from U.S. vendors, or platforms developed with U.S. RISC/UNIX technology, potential buyers should carefully check out the capabilities of the U.S. vendor standing behind a candidate Japanese offering. Table 6-2 is a rough list of vendors and suppliers to keep in mind when assessing platform options.

Table 6-2: Japanese UNIX Vendors in the U.S. Market

Vendor	Supplier
Hitachi	HP
Mitsubishi	HP
Oki Electric	HP
Fujitsu	Sun
Toshiba	Sun
Nihon Unisys	Sun
NEC	MIPs
Sony	MIPs

Hewlett-Packard: Most companies downsizing to open systems have found HP to be the best choice of hardware vendor. Dataquest measured HP's share as second to Sun in the 1991 worldwide workstation market (Sun was 29% to HP's 18% in the Dataquest survey), but the more recent *UNIXWORLD* December 1992 issue showed HP's UNIX revenues exceeding Sun's ($4.1 billion vs. $3.9 billion).[3] Moreover, HP has been the undisputed leader of the commercial multiuser RISC/UNIX market (important market for downsizing MIS managers) for several years—a market in which HP gained a dominant 48.6% share position in 1991, according to Aberdeen Group's February 1992 survey. The survey shows IBM trailing HP with only a 17.1% share, and (surprising to some) Sun with only a 7.1% share.

Since 1990, HP's UNIX revenues have grown at 30% according to Info Corp. HP records show that HP's midrange UNIX growth has been 51% in 1991 and 42% in 1992. But even a 30% growth rate (Info Corp.'s number) is 50% higher than the growth of the UNIX market as a whole. To achieve this type of performance, HP has

---

3. Wong, Carolyn W.C., "The Top 10 UNIX Companies," *UNIXWORLD,* Dec. 1992, 46–54.

stayed ahead of the pack in many product and service areas. Judging from the supportive comments made by companies interviewed for this book, HP's commercial UNIX success is here to stay.

HP is an example of the smart follower overtaking more complacent computer market leaders. IBM and DEC did not see as much to gain from moving to open systems. In fact, they saw the dawning of open systems as an impending threat to the stability of their installed base of customers. Their customers were locked into proprietary system environments, for which prices can be artificially inflated on vendor-provided hardware and software components, as well as support and system integration services. As to be expected, these two vendors spent substantial time in self-denial about the success of open systems. DEC's president (until mid-1992), Kenneth H. Olsen, once even referred to the UNIX operating system as "snake oil." During the time these vendors were waffling about commitment to UNIX, HP steadfastly developed the leading edge, commercially robust open systems that are taking the market by storm today. The two U.S. computer industry "leaders" are now playing catch up. As they do, they are undoubtedly realizing that building robustness into their UNIX systems equivalent to HP's is going to take time—time during which many satisfied HP customers will be saving money and enhancing their system functionality with HP platforms. HP's competitive advantages for today's downsizing customers are:

- **No lock-ins:** HP is considered by independent research companies as the most committed to open systems of any vendor. HP was the first vendor to ship an XPG3-compliant (X/OPEN branded) system. In addition to building standard compliant systems, HP is also a major force behind creating the standards themselves. The major standards organizations, including OSF, IEEE, X/OPEN, and SVID are actively supported by over 300 HP employees in numerous management and development roles. The system functionality incorporated by HP into its open systems platforms has come to be equivalent, if not superior, to many IBM and DEC proprietary systems.

- **Broadest line of system offerings with object code compatibility:** HP's product line is a continuum of object-compatible PA-RISC and HP-UX products from multi-user PC equivalents up to mainframe power systems (Figure 6-6). HP also offers workstations, Intel chip-based PCs, pocket computers, and X terminals. This array of products allows customers to obtain exactly the amount of computing power and functionality necessary for the traffic and applications running on their systems,

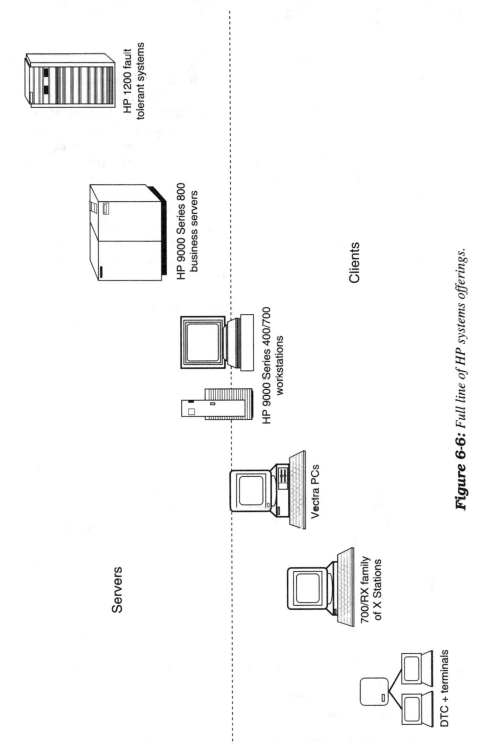

Servers

HP 1200 fault
tolerant systems

HP 9000 Series 800
business servers

HP 9000 Series 400/700
workstations

Clients

Vectra PCs

700/RX family
of X Stations

DTC + terminals

Figure 6-6: Full line of HP systems offerings.

while the compatibility among HP products allows for virtually unlimited switching of platforms, without software conversions or rewrites. Customers that would like to purchase from one vendor can order systems from HP to answer most, if not all, of their enterprise network system needs...and HP is enhancing this line of products at an annual price performance improvement of 60-70%. Even without new product introductions, HP's open systems product line breadth clearly exceeds competitors (Figure 6-7).

- **"Mainframe style" commercial robustness:** No open systems vendor can claim commercial robustness equivalent to mainframes today, but HP is the closest. As mentioned earlier, HP's system management technology has been accepted in open bidding to play the central role in OSF's distributed management environment, and HP is still building upon that base in new

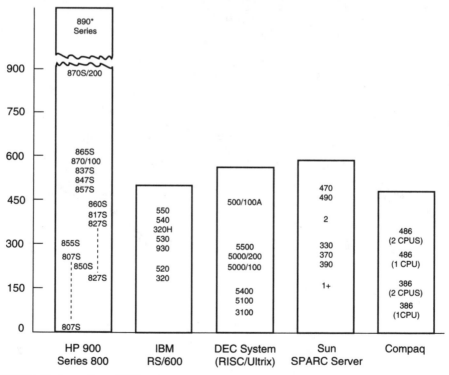

Series 890 supports a maximum of 4,500 users

Figure 6-7: *Major vendors open systems product lines.*

releases of HP's OpenView system management product. Also mentioned earlier was HP's robust high availability options for disk memory on-line backup and system switchover, raising HP system reliability from the already high 99.8% up to 99.995%. HP's systems are without a doubt the most reliable open systems in the industry.

- **The fastest machines in the industry:** In benchmark test after benchmark test, HP's systems have left competitor platforms in the dust on price performance. This price performance advantage is not a fluke. HP rolled the strategic dice in the early 80s and invested five long years in RISC architecture and system development before leading the industry with a RISC platform introduction in 1986. HP's RISC architecture is used in both HP's proprietary and open systems product lines. Today, HP's RISC technology has become fully developed and is providing superior dividends. It is unlikely that other vendors will be able to accelerate their learning curves in this technology without the inevitable costly slip-ups that have come to be known as standard fare when leading edge technologies are rushed to market before their time.

- **The closest to the most capable and influential third-party software providers:** The forward-looking mainframe software package vendors porting applications to UNIX have, for the most part, chosen HP as a strategic platform. The list of such software vendors includes Dun & Bradstreet, Computer Associates, Software AG, Cincom, IBI, and even IBM CICS.

HP has equity investments in two of the major relational database vendors, INFORMIX and Ingres, and is the highest volume platform for the largest relational database company in the U.S., Oracle. HP also has embarked on significant joint programs with Sybase. Together with these database vendors, HP is helping to define much of the future for commercial open systems computing.

It is unlikely that a superior open systems application or utility package will be introduced without being tuned to work effectively on HP. The drawing power that other leading platform vendors have had on ISVs in the past by virtue of their large market share positions, is true for HP today...and even more so. Since HP is drawing them into the open systems market, ISVs moving to HP view the total open systems movement as their business opportunity and increase their software development

efforts proportionately. Leaders in the world of software package
development are moving in droves to open systems platforms,
and the vast majority are targeting the open systems market
leader, HP. Already HP can boast over 3,500 applications available on their commercial UNIX platform alone.

- **Customer service and support:** Only HP can claim eight
  straight years of being ranked #1 by Datapro, a well-known
  independent research company, in U.S. customer support satisfaction surveys. The rankings were taken as an average across
  five categories: Maintenance effectiveness, Maintenance respon-
  siveness, Troubleshooting, Documentation, and Education.

- **Longevity:** HP has grown at a steady 20% pace as a company
  for most of the fifty years of its existence. During that time, HP
  has always maintained healthy profits. Even during the last
  couple of years when most competitors, including IBM, Unisys,
  DEC, Compaq, and Sequent, have experienced either quarterly
  or annual losses, HP has held strong, and in fact, has demonstrated excellent corporate stability with an increase of nearly
  13% in revenues and a 40–50% increase in net profits during
  the first two quarters of 1992. HP's outlook is also excellent
  given the long list of competitive advantages in its open systems
  product lines, and HP's major share position in that market.

- **HP has products localized for Japan:** Japanese customer
  interest has not fallen on deaf ears at HP. HP has been making a
  series of strategic investments in localizing all open systems
  and client/server software for Japan starting in 1991. HP
  expects to increase Japan open systems revenues by over 60%
  annually and exceed $500 million in 1996. If you work at a Jap-
  anese company and haven't already...perhaps you should have
  a chat with HP or YHP about your commercial system needs.

How About Biting the Bullet and Moving to Real Client/Server?

First of All, What Is Real Client/Server?

Client/server is one of those terms everyone apparently has license to define as they wish. Venders are being accused of slapping the term onto existing products to enhance their marketability. Research companies are also doing their bit to muddy the waters with varying interpretations. Forrester Research Inc. defines client/server "for the record" with these words in their 1991 report entitled "Re-Sizing Client/Server:"[1]

> For the record, Forrester defines client/server computing as "clients and servers cooperating to do a job." This architecture is differentiated from past attempts at distributed processing by its reliance on the intelligent PC, Mac, or UNIX workstation on the user's desk. Simply stated, application processing is split between a client and a single server.

Everything clear now? Does this mean you cannot have two servers working with one client on the same application? What if just the user interface is left on the client and the application code

---

1. Forrester Research, Inc., "Resizing Client/Server," *Focus*, 1991, 1.

remains on the single server? Is this client/server? Let's try the definition provided by Gartner Group in their May 29, 1992 report entitled "Client/Server Architecture: A Management Perspective."[2]

> Client/server is the splitting of an application into tasks which are performed on separate computers, one of which is a programmable workstation, e.g., a PC (if a PC only emulates an IBM 3270 terminal, we sometimes refer to this as "brain dead" client/server). More commonly, the term client/server brings to mind PCs on a local area network, which is linked to one or more servers and to a mainframe as resources.

Any better? Client/server technology is evolving so rapidly that new insights are brought to the meaning of client/server distributed processing concepts with every new product introduced. So far we have not yet seen the product or products that the world can acclaim as "having defined client/server." When these products arrive, the license for free definition of the term will expire, and computer industry pundits will become busy with a term for the next generation of computing.

Let me take a stab at defining client/server for use in this book, since the license has yet to expire.

Definition

Client/server is: two or more computers working together across a network to provide users with a user-friendly interface residing on the desktop, application functionality shared across multiple machines as required, and database capabilities (usually of the relational variety) on the more powerful non-desktop machine or machines (servers).

Objectives

Client/server systems are designed to distribute functionality and compute burden across a network of computers to:

- Provide the user with ease of use, quick response, and access to useful data and applications

2. Gartner Group RAS Services, *Client/Server Architecture: A Management Perspective*, May 29, 1992, 6.

- Effectively use all the MIPs available in the network to provide the above functionality, while

  - Minimizing network traffic, and

  - Maximizing system management, and system development ease

You may feel that I have not improved on the above definitions, or that I have only narrowed the definition to a very specific type of client/server computing. Let me share with you a framework developed by HP's internal system development teams, who are struggling with creating client/server systems today. Perhaps it will bring the definition more to life.

A Client/Server Development Framework

The essence of the framework is the partitioning of distributed system software logic into discrete modules, and the defining of standard interfaces between the modules. This allows for discrete portions of a client/server system to be developed and maintained separately, located remotely or locally, and accessed seamlessly (the user does not need to know where the modules are located to engage them). The modules defined by HP's internal team are contained in Figure 7-1. Let me outline the characteristics of each one and suggest where they might reside in a distributed network.

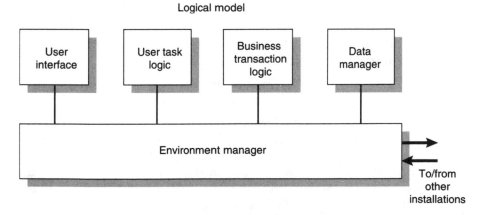

Figure 7-1: HP's internally developed client/server development framework.

1. **User interface:** This part creates the "face" of the computer. It is responsible for guiding the user in some way (ASCII text, image, or sound) to provide appropriate input for the task or tasks at hand. The most popular interfaces today are Graphical User Interfaces (GUIs) which present data and options for the user to choose, carry out limited checks on user input (complains, for instance, if a user tries to spell a name in numbers instead of letters), help format user input (justification, upshifting, wrap-around, truncation, and patterning), and control the interface presentation (window size/resize, speed of display, etc.). A main objective is to provide a consistent user interface across applications that is so easy to use that it is intuitive (requires little to no training for the first-time user).

2. **User task logic:** This is the intelligence behind the computer face. It directs the user interface to present choices, data, and otherwise interact with the user so it can build "transaction packets" for corresponding with the various applications residing in the distributed network. For instance, the user task logic might stop an order processing clerk as a new customer order is input and ask the clerk for data necessary for completing a credit check (required for all new customers). In addition to sending order entry information across the network to the server, the user task logic would also send a credit check package to a separate application designed to access outside credit check databases. The user task logic in the framework is defined as:

   • Event-driven (it is initiated when specified conditions are met). Simple conditions are, for instance, the click of a mouse or a key entry from the keyboard. More complex conditions would be the entry of a "new" customer, or the input of other variables significant to the task at hand.

   • Able to fully edit user choices and data, in the context of the application (context-sensitive help).

   • Able to manage the interaction between the user interface and the business transaction logic module (described next) by building and sending transaction packets to the business transaction logic (usually across the network), receiving and interpreting results, and communicating results to the user through the user interface.

   • Able to work with standard protocols in all interaction with the two other modules.

- Able to provide limited security, by presenting only data and choices appropriate for the security status of the user.

3. **Business transaction logic:** The business transaction logic is on the receiving end of the transaction packages sent by the user task logic. It carries out non-database functions that are "shared" across multiple users. For instance, the new customer order transaction package sent in the above example could be placed in temporary storage until authorization is received from the credit check. Time limits could be imposed by the business transaction logic to poll the credit application if no authorization is received within a certain period of time. Depending on the credit status, appropriate authorization messages could also be sent by the business transaction logic back to the user and perhaps to the sales manager assigned to the customer as well. The most straightforward job for this logic module would be to interact with the data manager (explained next) to create, retrieve, update, and delete data. The business logic would also ensure the consistency and integrity of the data in the context of the application and task at hand. Furthermore, the business logic also interprets data (e.g., expands codes into text, summarizes or derives information) for responding to the user (or requester...it may be another machine on the network).

4. **Data manager:** What more is there left to do? In fact, a lot. The data manager module not only carries out the physical storage and retrieval of data in one or multiple databases (and other data storage areas), it provides for physical table integrity and allows for recovery of data from incomplete processing. It also manages concurrent access to data by multiple users (what if two users change the same file at the same time?), and manages interactions with printers and information gateways, such as EDI. The database manager conducts further security checks, allowing access only to files authorized for the category of user requesting.

5. **Environment manager:** This module closely approximates the "network" in traditional computer terminology. It loads and starts the other modules (and assures they are running appropriately), balances the network traffic load by sending network control routing messages to the appropriate network components (acts as the agent for sending such messages from the system manager), and of course, provides a standard interface among the other logical modules.

So what does this division of computing labor do for the system? It provides many of the benefits (or client/server objectives) described in the beginning of this chapter!

- "Ease of use and quick response" to user inputs can be provided by placing the user interface module on the desktop. The level of intelligence in the immediate response (from generating "beeps" for inputting format errors up to querying users concerning the content of input data) can be enhanced by placing the user task logic on the desktop as well.

- "Access to useful data" can be provided to more users, and in a more efficient way because of the added intelligence in the database (relational database technology) for conducting queries defined interactively by the user. More importantly, network and compute bottlenecks are mitigated by the distribution of tasks to the desktop, freeing up compute power throughout the system so that all users have more CPU time to conduct database queries. The same is true with respect to accessing applications residing in business transaction logic on the server.

- "Minimizing network traffic and maximizing system management and support ease" is a balancing act achieved through careful analysis to optimize the distribution of application logic across the network. To demonstrate this point, consider the type of system design that would, say, simply minimize network traffic. An answer that would push traffic minimization to the extreme, would be to pack the desktop with MIPs and memory, and stuff as much as possible (if not all) of the logical modules onto the desktop for carrying out both individual and shared tasks. This, of course, would be an expensive solution because of duplication of MIPs (at least until MIPs really become free). It would also result in a system management nightmare when implementing software updates and other fixes, because every client machine would have to be adjusted for every change.

In the host/terminal configuration, we have a nightmare of the opposite dimension. Since all the logical modules reside on the server (usually the mainframe), software fixes and upgrades are less complex (only requiring a change code on the server) but serious bottlenecks in the network and at the server CPU abound, and undermine the overall effectiveness of the system. The division of compute labor in the client/server framework allow us to strike a happy medium...shared data and application code can reside on the more powerful server or servers, and application and data for promptly reacting to user input can reside on the desktop. Network traffic is minimized by disassociating the server from the user's every keystroke, and system adjustments and updates can take place on the small number of servers, rather than the thousands of clients (the need to change standard user interfaces is less frequent).

- "Maximize development ease." Once the system code is broken into the five discrete modules with standard interfaces (described previously), numerous system and software development efficiencies come into play. Teams can be assigned to each module and can work in parallel so that a system can be completed in one-fourth to one-fifth the time, compared to sequential development programs on the mainframe. This is in fact the "magic" behind many of the open systems system integrator claims heard today about such feats as "rapid prototyping in three weeks" and "system development in one-fourth the time."

Division into teams also promotes the development of specialized expertise within different sections of the MIS department. Team members can focus on becoming specialists in one area (say GUIs, servers, databases, or networking) rather than having to keep up with technologies and disciplines across the board. This is especially helpful for bringing mainframe specialists quickly up to speed in the new distributed environment.

The division of code into modules also allows for much code reuse. The user interface, for instance, can be the same for all applications. To some extent, the user task logic can be consistent across the system desktop devices as well. Subroutines developed for one application can often be accessed by another application residing on the same or a different server, because of the standardization of module interfaces.

Finally, system maintenance is also enhanced because adjustments can be made to one module (and often to one portion of the module) without impacting the rest of the system. Most changes, in fact, will be transparent to (unnoticed by) the user because the user interface and interface logic will rarely be touched.

The client/server framework needs to be adjusted to some degree depending on the nature of the computing work. Decision support systems, for instance, often need to interact with the user based on the most recent information available at the server. For instance, if information for only certain regions of the country is available on the server at the time the user logs on, the user would like to know that before making data requests. If the user interface logic resides, as suggested above, on the client, the user will not know the database status until after making a first request. If, on the other hand, the user interface logic is on the server, it can relay up-to-date information to the user about the status of data residing in the system. A drawback to this option, however, is that control of the user interface remains on the server throughout the session, often leading to excessive network traffic. A workaround to this problem, developed by the HP internal team, is to have the server shoot the user interface logic over to the client when the user logs in. In this way, the client user task logic is up to date, and the user interface can be completely managed by the client machine.

This framework may sound quite straightforward to many readers, in fact, I believe the concept has been around for years in various industries. Walk into a restaurant, for instance, and you can find many similarities between how the waitress attends to your needs and how the client system, equipped with user interface and user task logic capability, responds to your requests. The waitress first offers you a menu of options for dinner. If you ask for something not on the menu, she will direct you back to the menu to make another selection (user interface and user task logic). If you insist, she may go back to the kitchen (the restaurant counterpart to the server with information on the availability of services (applications) and raw materials (data), to see if your special request can be filled (business transaction logic and data manager). She also can exercise some limited security functions. If she notices that you are so drunk that you cannot speak properly, she can have you expelled from the restaurant and refuse you access to restaurant service.

Without the waitress, the cook would have to make rounds of the tables, which would be quite inefficient, and certainly cause bot-tlenecks back in the kitchen. Today's computing choices, (1) host/terminal, or (2) distributed client/server, could perhaps be described using this analogy as either (1) hire a superhuman cook (mainframe) who can make rounds of the tables and cook the food at lightning speed, or (2) use mere mortals and accomplish the same (or better) through a client/server division of labor.

Where Are the Tools to Create This Client/Server World?

There are in fact, quite a few tools on the market that purport to supporting client/server development efforts. The majority of these tools, however, limit their scope to CLIENT system development, i.e., the user interface, application logic, and server interface.

Client Development Tools

Tools should be selected depending upon the type of client/server development project at hand, e.g., how much of the graphical user interface needs to be created from scratch, how much of the application logic is to be distributed among computers, etc. Here is a list of the more common features provided by client server tools for creating client software.

- **User interface design:** Tools range from those adept at developing terminal-style interactive interfaces with dialog editing, to interactive screen painters for Graphical User Interfaces (GUIs) fronting new and existing applications. The GUI tools vary in their support of on-screen graphical objects such as soft buttons, drop down instruction boxes, and menu lists. Some also provide custom control capabilities for changing the shape or color of the buttons and other GUI fixtures.

- **Application logic:** As pointed out in the discussion of user task logic and application logic in the internal HP model, the notion of what makes up application logic on the client can vary considerably by vendor. Application logic tools contain "scripting languages" of basically two flavors: procedural (Powersoft's Powerbuilder and Within Technology's Realizer) and event-driven. Procedural application logic languages are structured along the lines of traditional sequenced programming languages (Cobol and Fortran). Event-driven scripting languages are often equipped with limited object-oriented capabilities for linking applications and data. These tools use extensions of C, or in the case of Choreographer, create their own language.

- **Code management:** Basic facilities for organizing team code development efforts are also necessary. Client/server tools often include code library, version management, and configuration control to keep all programmers in lock-step as the client application is developed.

- **Compatibility:** U.S. desktop client operating systems are more standardized than those in Japan. U.S. PCs are either IBM PC-compatible or they are Apple Macintosh, whereas Japanese PCs can belong to a variety of different proprietary worlds. Most U.S. development tools work in one U.S. environment or the other, and a few straddle both, such as Blyth Software Inc.'s Omnis/5. Few of these tools have been localized to work in the fragmented Japanese PC environment.

- **Server interface features:** Client tools also distinguish themselves by the server interface features they provide. The server interface portion of the client application receives calls from the application logic, translates them into interprocess communications protocols, and sends requests to the server. Powerbuilder, Choreographer, and Easel all support multiple SQL database instructions for carrying out this function. Choreographer and Easel also support LU6.2 protocols for communicating peer-to-peer in the IBM environment. In addition, Ellipse supports multiple servers, heterogeneous databases, and two-phase commit. Other tools, such as Realizer and Visual Basic are not equipped with server interface functionality, and therefore are better suited to less interactive client application development.

Server Development Tools

Server application development tools available today rarely provide development environments for true client/server application development. Most offer little more for client/server development than the standard distributed midrange and workstation system development functions. Two vendors, however, are delivering tools that are designed especially for development on both clients and servers: Andersen Computing's Foundation for Cooperative Processing, and Texas Instrument's IEF CASE Offering. Let me briefly describe the type of capabilities these tools offer.

- Integrated development environment for GUI, client, and server application development. All of the application components are placed in one central repository and are generated by the same set of tools, to ensure consistency and compatibility of application modules developed for a client/server system.

- Application generation tools that not only create code for the individual platform, but also construct the interactive communication components for cross-system client and server interaction. Much of the system management capabilities are also generated automatically, including shared data, security, and recovery unit management.

- Major system protocols are handled by the development tools as well. For instance, data translations between C and Cobol programs, and between EBCDIC and ASCII code, are carried out automatically. The client GUI is often portable to a variety of clients, and message delivery and platform access functions can be developed for an increasing number of client and server types.

These tools are basically an extension of the I-CASE tools (discussed in Chapter 5) with enhanced capabilities for developing applications that run on multiple heterogeneous interacting platforms. The development task is complex for client/server applications, and I am sure it has been extremely difficult for software vendors to create these client/server CASE tools. The more comprehensive tools are new and few companies have completed true client/server application development programs using them. Companies looking into them may want to check them out thoroughly on a few small pilot projects before risking their mission critical operations.

Why Isn't Everyone Already Using Client/Server Architecture?

First of all, the technologies for implementing client/server are just becoming available today. Moreover, even though productivity tools are making the transition easier, major changes of the scale discussed in this book often meet resistance from MIS staff and other managers. Here is a sampling of what I heard during interviews with downsizing companies in September of 1992:

- Software developers who have worked on IBM systems for many years view the distributed system languages and tools as "beneath" them. They view PCs as "toys" and often opt to switch companies if their MIS shop chooses to downsize. By moving to a mainframe shop, they can continue to use the "high caliber" mainframe skills they have cultivated over the years.

The mainframe proprietary environment and the freewheeling UNIX workstation and PC environments represent two very different cultures. UNIX experts, who are new to the data center, often need to learn the rigors of security and data integrity before they become truly effective. Until they do, they are regarded as the "hackers" MIS data center managers have been trying to restrain all these years. At the same time, there is a lot that mainframe Cobol programmers must learn before they can be useful in the distributed environment. It is often difficult to force people to learn something they consider beneath them, and the fact that what they have to learn is also difficult makes it impossible for some.

- What is so difficult to learn? Many of the opportunities described in this book represent paradigm shifts of various magnitudes and gyrations. The concept of developing programs in parallel rather than sequentially, the method of establishing standard protocol interfaces between parts of the same application, the ability to access parts of the system across a network rather than across a mainframe, and the accompanying need to ensure transaction data integrity across multiple systems and databases, etc., are all uncharted waters for many data shops today. This book is an attempt to bring to light some of the more navigable areas, and some of the tools that are available to make the waters easier to travel.

  Another important hurdle is mastering the basic language skills themselves. Programmers who want to be effective on the systems side of the distributed environment need to learn, for instance, the memory management techniques of the C language. C is a language with which a developer can easily destroy a machine's memory by inadvertently dropping a punctuation mark. Another important difference, especially in working with GUIs, is the existence of event-driven, pre-emptive interruptions. This is a world in which any program can be derailed by another program operating at a higher priority.

The ways which downsizing companies are dealing with the difficult issues of changing MIS culture are as varied as their company cultures. Some painstakingly retrain their staff at the pace their staff can move, and shift the system over with similar timing. Others decide to pull the plug on the mainframe and change the whole MIS department at the same time. Still others are able to avoid retraining their staff in C and use 4GL tools to mask them from the vagaries of the system. No matter how it is done, the process is not "business as usual." The next section tells how a company in northern Vermont managed to change their MIS (and company) culture during the downsizing transition.

Simmonds Precision Aircraft Systems

What type of company culture do you think your company would have if the company's prosperity was inextricably linked with a government defense budget that ebbed and flowed with the political winds of the country? What if, during boom war years your company grew to 2,200, but as peace arrived, 2/3 of your employees had to be jettisoned to slim the ranks to 800?

The laws of the corporate land in such grim circumstances take on odd twists and turns. Instead of survival of the fittest, it sometimes becomes survival of the least conspicuous. Managers who take risks and go out on a limb for the company are offering top management a branch to prune for better achieving cost reduction goals. Few innovative ideas are forthcoming in this type of environment, and few decisions are made without getting approval from the whole chain of command. In short, the company becomes tied up in a bureaucratic straitjacket and managers become risk-averse in the extreme.

Such was the case at Simmonds Precision, a major producer of fuel measurement/management systems. Simmonds is a proud and capable company founded by Sir Oliver Simmonds, a pioneer in the aerospace industry. Some of the most innovative patents from the early 1940s for fuel gauging are among the assets of this company, a company whose products are found on virtually every aircraft, air shuttle, and spacecraft launched from western nations.

Three years ago, BFGoodrich Aerospace acquired Simmonds and provided a long needed return to what managers in the company refer to as "entrepreneurial spirit." This is a story of what that transition meant to Simmonds management and especially to the MIS team.

Early in the process, BFGoodrich assembled a top management team that was committed to making "the necessary changes." The organization structure was also reshuffled to focus Simmonds management talents on meeting customer needs, rather than on overcoming internal coordination barriers. The previous product/function organization was replaced by Strategic Business Units (SBUs) defined as Military, Commercial, and Sensor businesses. Additional focus on building a strong Simmonds commercial business was seen as a way for gradually releasing Simmonds from the ups and downs of the government defense budget.

It was just after the BFGoodrich acquisition that Dick Wright was appointed MIS director at Simmonds. His appointment was a dramatic departure from the past. Rather than appointing an information systems specialist, BFGoodrich chose a manager with skills for the new environment. Mr. Wright had business expertise and a demonstrated track record for leading cross-organizational development programs.

Mr. Wright formed a cross-functional team to investigate the effectiveness of information systems. The team soon found that the existing Simmonds systems were not geared for supporting the new strategic initiatives. Four islands of technology had grown up within Simmonds over time: a DEC island for engineering, an IBM island for financial and administration applications, a Wang island for word processing, and an HP island for manufacturing. Not only was little information shared among the systems, minimal information was shared among the organizations each system supported. The team was amazed to see that even the computer vendors reflected this mentality. Vendors focused their efforts almost completely on the islands using their equipment and had little knowledge of the overall IS needs of the company. The disjointed information systems structure made it all the more difficult to become aggressive in bidding on the newer projects, for which cost data needed to be collected cross-functionally, which meant crossing "islands" at Simmonds.

It was clear to the team and the company managers that this was not the type of problem to go after with a band-aid approach. Rather, it required major surgery on the corporate culture to re-inject entrepreneurial spirit into the veins of the company. It also required a major transformation of MIS staff into true supporters of end-user computing to make them instrumental agents in accomplishing the company's business objectives.

The first symbol of change for Simmonds was the replacement of the most bureaucratically entrenched management members. That alone raised morale within the company considerably, according to Mr. Wright. The reorganization into strategic business units was the second move. Flesh was added to the bones of the new organization structural with the introduction of new budgeting and performance measurement systems designed to focus management attention on the needs of their customers, and away from internal turf battles. Decision-making was decentralized to managers who were closer to the organizational levers instrumental for generating true customer value. Department managers who felt uneasy about their expanded freedom in decision-making and cost allocation were reassured by the new management team that it was okay to take calculated risks and make mistakes, as long as the communication links were kept open for sharing experiences and, in the worst case, minimizing damages. Management drove home their cultural change messages in meeting after meeting, both in groups and in one-on-one conversations. The employees really knew the company had changed when they were told ahead of time (unprecedented!) about some of the most difficult decisions a management can make—layoffs.

As part of the overall change program, Mr. Wright and his team were asked to map out three-year strategic and one-year tactical plans for transforming MIS. Included in the plans was to be a methodology for billing MIS services to Simmonds' new SBUs and functional departments so that all managers would know where their MIS charges were going. Mr. Wright constructed a culture change program aimed at converting his team from an MIS "production group into a professional organization." He explains, "We will have no need for traditional programmers anymore...they will all become User Computing Analysts...in fact, if MIS really does the job appropriately, we will be out of a job." Mr. Wright means of course they will be out of a programming job and will be out mixing with end-user customers, acting as businesses generators, and leveraging both their information systems skills and newly acquired business experience and understanding.

This new orientation of the company and the MIS organization opened the door to considering alternative methods of computing. Mr. Wright asked three hardware vendors to bid on the development of an information network to tie the company together as an integrated whole. None of the forthcoming vendor proposals appeared completely appropriate to the team, so they developed their own system vision in line with Simmonds' needs. Mr. Wright then asked for systems integration bids to put it all together. Ironically, IBM won the systems integration project, a project to unplug an IBM mainframe and replace it with an HP server.

The new vision (Figure 7-2) is called Internet (after the famous TCP/IP network linking UNIX users around the world). In true Internet style, it links all of Simmonds' islands of automation together. The IBM mainframe finance and administration programs were replaced with software from Computer Financial Services (CFS). The CFS packages are now to be integrated with manufacturing applications and placed on an HP server running HP's proprietary MPE operating system (MPE includes sufficient open systems interfaces to be considered more open than many UNIX systems on the market today). The DEC VAX system is to be linked to the HP server, as well

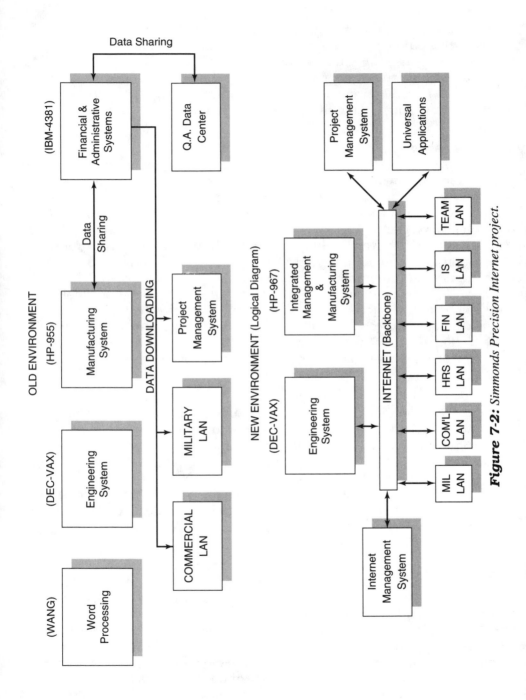

Figure 7-2: *Simmonds Precision Internet project.*

as to LANs throughout the company. Mr. Wright expects the DEC platform to be the next target of opportunity.

The move to the new vision will bring not only a new perspective on life to Simmonds, but also substantial cost savings. Mr. Wright compares the IBM 4381 mainframe to old oil burner technology. "Unplugging the mainframe and making the accompanying adjustments in MIS staff (43 employees in March of 1991 to 20 in January 1993) will cut MIS costs by over 30%...and it will also usher in a new era of flexibility. We will not only be able to get the information necessary for making timely and competitive bids. We can cut the database any way we want...by business unit, by part, and by customer...all without investing a lot of MIS time. Even with reduced staffing, we expect to decrease MIS operation hours to five days with lights out at night...that is a big change from the 24-hour, 7-day operation required with IBM."

Mr. Wright believes that none of this would have been possible without the more supportive BFGoodrich environment. He received letters of encouragement from division and business management when the MIS challenge was upped to switching over the system in one year instead of three. Embedded in the encouragement was another, even more important message. The management team said that they were ready to do anything in their power to help the team achieve the accelerated goal. The team members feel they are partially out on a limb, but instead of it being a limb for management to lop off, it is a limb of future growth, one that top management is ready to nurture into full bloom.

Tables 7-1 and 7-2 are the MIS team's charts for describing the MIS transformation Simmonds is going through. Which environment do you think best describes MIS in your company...the "Mainframe" or the "New?"

A major non-technical obstacle in moving to distributed systems and client/server architectures is management and employee fear of the potency with which information systems can restructure an organization. An effective EDI event-driven order processing system can eliminate scores of jobs in the invoicing department, as managers realize that there is no need for employees to compare purchase orders with bills of lading, and invoices, the computer systems do it automatically. A great swath can also be cut out of the middle management ranks with effective decision support systems. Managers whose major jobs were to filter information up (progress reports, issues, and concerns) and downward (corporate policies, goals, and programs) find themselves struggling to find other areas of value added to justify their existence.

**Table 7-1: Environment Comparison:
Mainframe vs. Downsized Environment at Simmonds Precision***

Company Organizational Impact	
Mainframe	New Environment
Central control	Shared control
Less flexible	More flexible, dynamic systems
Long product life cycle	Short product life cycle
Long business application life span	Shorter business application life span (will stretch over time)
Difficulty of change hinders on-going changes, improvement	Ease of modification (e.g., tools database) supports improved processes
User support less intricate and complicated	User support more complicated by SW and HW spread and multiple interconnections
Centralized resource, processing capability	Shared data, vulnerable, less IS control
Very little customer involvement	High level of customer involvement

User Involvement	
Mainframe	New Environment
Less	More
Backup: IS responsibility	Backup: shared responsibility
File Sync: IS responsibility	File Sync: User plays active role
IS has applications control responsibility under typical batch	User has some responsibility for applications controls (e.g., file access)
IS does file maintenance, archiving, etc.	User shares in file maintenance, archiving, etc.
Nominal (if any) technological literacy	Some additional technological literacy

Cost Technology	
Mainframe	New Environment
Costs in large increments; start-up high	Scalable costs in smaller increments; start-up high, depending on technology
Limited to a basic cost allocations system	Allows closer control by tying IS support costs to business functions supported
Static, dedicated resources	Mobile, re-usable resources
Leased operating system software, maintenance, recurring costs (market does not necessarily work to lower costs)	Operating system software bought outright, maintenance, recurring costs (market mechanism lowers costs over time)
No real, direct relationship between costs, service, and investment	Easier for business person (user) to understand

* Source: Simmonds Precision

Information Week devoted a cover story[3] to what they referred to as the "horizontal, flattened organization." Motorola Inc.'s government electronics group is highlighted in the article as a $700 million business that has changed "just about every aspect of how it does business, including all standard processes: new tools, new systems, and new training...though the size of the business is about the same as it was when the reorganization started four years ago, there are fewer employees, about 5,000 now compared with 8,000 then." Motorola also changed the mission of its MIS department to support this change. Instead of calling it "IS," they have now named it Computer Integrated Design and Manufacturing (CIDM), and instead of a chief information officer, the CIDM is run by a steering committee of business and technology heads.

Not all companies embarking on downsizing are planning a complete revamp of their organizations. Nevertheless, changes in IS can open a Pandora's box for the very middle managers who are asked to consider the pros and cons of IS proposals. Job-threatening changes in the information systems structure are not likely to be approved by the middle ranks, and top management may not have insights into the reasons why some forward-looking IS proposals are rejected by their otherwise trustworthy subordinates.

3. Pepper, Jon, "The Horizontal Organization," *Information Week,* Aug.17, 1992, 32–40.

**Table 7-2: IS Organization in New Downsized Environment
at Simmonds Precision***

Business Interactions

Must understand business process, workflow

Must have excellent communications skills and literacy in the business

Will participate in and must understand strategic goals and plans of the business

Must understand users' expectations (real needs)

Must market and sell IS services

Must understand formal and informal needs of customer

Must be proactive in providing solutions for business processes and productivity
   improvements

Must provide the business organization with assistance and focus that are relevant and
   reflective of Simmonds' business needs

Must perform ongoing assessment of IS vs. business requirements (IS is always in
   support of business needs)

Consulting Functions

Define customers' business expectations in practical, accomplishable terms

Provide "road map" to data (corporate)

Act as facilitator in developmental process

Adjust role based upon customer

Provide IS strategic plan and tactical plan to support the business plans

Provide industry-type knowledge of business processes and systems used in similar
   businesses (customer market segment)

Determine availability and appropriateness of business applications for the company

* Source: Simmonds Precision

Technology Offerings

Exposing customer to technological advances available in marketplace and potentially to them if the technologies are business-relevant (business drives technology search and choice)

Analyzing current business processes for opportunities to improve:
- lower labor cost
- higher effectiveness

Providing recommendations for use and distribution of technology already in house (via migration, technology optimization, e.g., E-mail)

Providing technological infrastructure for business organization

Providing direct, precise technical information to customers regarding technology capabilities in response to user/customer questions

Providing rapid development of solutions and applications

Planning the total IS environment

Planning the PC expenditures and ownership, taking control of PCs on the network

---

IS Department Structure/Evolution

Smaller, more versatile and flexible (fewer specialists, more generalists)

More interactive (internal/external)

More sophisticated in understanding business needs

Oriented to view IS as a service function (spending someone else's money)

Committed to develop and maintain customer orientation, sense of partnership

More horizontal (less top-heavy, bureaucratic; more team-minded, responsive) valuing
- interpersonal skills
- matrix relationships
- interactive teams
- new framework/mindset

"Empowered" to provide customer satisfaction within pre-determined parameters

What Do You Do with a Downsized Client/Server System?

Decision Support

Twenty-five percent of Japanese companies surveyed by HP research in 1992 said that they were planning to invest in decision support systems within two years. An astounding 52% claimed that they would invest in a decision support system in the next five years. Clearly decision support has captured the imagination of corporate Japan. An MIS manager from a major Japanese ball bearing manufacturer echoed this interest in a recent interview. He comments, "Decision support systems are necessary in almost every division of this company...all management teams need easy-to-understand data about their operations."

A Japanese financial industry giant recently took the lead in implementing downsized decision support systems for numerous planning, financial tracking, auditing, and policy setting organizations within its head office. Before the change, the Integrated Planning Office (the department championing the change) would make requests using SAS tools on IBM mainframes residing several cities away to analyze such trends as the erosion of direct deposit accounts caused by changes in savings account interest rates. Answers would often take four hours to process. In their minds, this was no way to run a major financial institution in an era of deregulation and discontinuous change. They were witnessing industry convulsions rendering many of their U.S. and Japanese competitors unprofitable, and in some areas, such as U.S. Savings and Loan institutions, undermining the viability of a whole segment of the financial sector.

The Assistant Director of the Integrated Planning Office is well-versed in both business and information technology issues. In fact, he has personally created many of the algorithms used at the bank for analyzing shifts in the business environment. Under his leadership and the direction of an IS-enlightened second lieutenant, users banded together and launched their own project (coordinating with the traditional IS leadership) to solve their information problems. In early 1990 they launched a System Development Team, consisting of both end users and system development members, ranging in computer expertise from employees who knew computers from touching the keyboard to others who had considerable development experience. Strict evaluation criteria for selecting different system components were defined by the team and an assessment of potential vendors was carried out over several months. Mounting dissatisfaction with the traditional host/terminal configuration led the team to decide on a vendor with strong downsizing, open systems and support credentials, YHP (Yokogawa Hewlett-Packard, HP's Japanese arm).

Several members from YHP then joined the team and helped develop a distributed decision support system for meeting the needs of the numerous and varied headquarters functions. The system was designed to pull down appropriate segments of the terabyte mainframe database to local servers for users to access for day-to-day activities and analysis. Software was selected both to meet the challenges of the analysis tasks, and to match the programming skill levels of the end users. HP worked with the other software providers to provide training to the company's support team and end users on UNIX, LANs, database use, and analysis tools. Three months after the contract with YHP had been signed the system was up and running!

How could it be built so fast? For one thing, the system was assembled using software application packages in a very straightforward way. Since SAS had already developed a version of their analytical tools for UNIX, the company simply bought SAS versions for all the new UNIX servers on each floor. SAS is appropriate for seasoned programmers requiring fine data granularity in their analysis, but it is generally too complex for the less experienced or more casual user. Additional software tools, reflecting a variety of programming skill levels and analytical features, were therefore purchased to meet the broader range of user needs within the headquarter departments. These additional tools included Information Builders, Inc.'s FOCUS for database segmentation and Access Technology's 20/20 for spreadsheet analysis on the server, Japanese word processing (Ichitaro), and PC spreadsheet software (Ashisuto Calc) on laptops (space saving was also a high priority), and an HP E-Mail system on the network. The servers are connected by TCP/IP and include Network File Server (NFS) utilities.

One important challenge that was not quite so straightforward was the orchestration of multiple software and hardware vendors' activities during system development. This was achieved by conducting weekly meetings of the seven major hardware and software providers. HP chaired the meetings, during which system issues were reviewed and responsible vendors were assigned to investigate.

The other important constituency to manage was the users. Nothing can undermine a change program more quickly than untrained or apathetic users wasting equipment and system time, and eventually bad-mouthing the project team's efforts. With the roll-out of the new system, training was made mandatory for all users and rules were set to promote usage. If, for instance, SAS was not accessed by a user for six months, or the PC laptop software was not used for three months, user access was denied. Moreover, passwords were changed every three months.

Now that the system is in place, headquarters is beginning to realize the true power of the system they have built. At a time when major financial institutions are hurting from over-extended loan portfolios, relational database technology allows them to track the bad loan status of each branch in infinite detail, and identify problem cases for close investigation. Furthermore, business opportunities are now brought to light by comparing fund flow data from communications carriers (NTT) with the bank's own fund flows in specific regions, cities, or even districts. Areas in which funds are flowing to competitors can be singled out through this analysis for implementation of special strategic initiatives, including temporary promotions and enhanced services to major commercial customers in the immediate area. Pity the financial institutions competing against this IS technology leader. This financial services powerhouse can direct nationwide resources at a moment's notice to shadow their every move!

The managers who championed the change to downsized systems radiate satisfaction when talking about the enhanced functionality and reduced hardware and maintenance costs, but expressions are less sanguine when discussing software licensing fees. The second lieutenant mentioned earlier exclaims "Downsizing is not really downsizing, as long as software vendors don't adjust their prices to reflect the realities of the distributed environment." Since license fees for many application packages are set by CPU, placing these applications on each floor server has raised software costs by several orders of magnitude. He is looking forward to a time when software companies will agree to concurrent user licensing...a utility already available from HP (called NETLS). NETLS passes out licenses across the network to each logged on user, up to the number of licenses owned by the company. Once that number is exceeded, either the last user is refused a license (until one is freed up by another user), or the software vendor is called to expand the number of licenses in the contract.

Another area in which the project managers have some misgivings is networking bandwidth—not enough was installed at the outset. Now that the system is a success, traffic on the network has grown exponentially. They are currently trying to connect more users through FDDI links and are running head on into system networking problems that could have been avoided by taking corrective measures during the first phases of installation...just another one of the many things to "decide about decision support" when moving to distributed system topologies.

How About Making Engineering Concurrent?

Leviton Mfg.

How much rework is generated because engineers and managers need to see and touch the end-product before they can be sure it is what they really want? What if they could be provided a sample from day one that they could adjust at will? How much rework would that eliminate? Quite a lot, according managers at Leviton Mfg., a privately-owned producer of electric wiring devices. They have recently downsized their engineering design system to gain this capability for their faster moving businesses. The program has been such a success that the Assistant VP of Engineering who led the change, Dennis Oddsen, finds little free time on his schedule. He is now in demand across the country to share his downsizing experiences with other forward looking companies.

Leviton owns a major portion of the electrical wiring device market in the U.S. and around the globe. Wiring devices have been such a standardized product that Leviton's product life cycles have historically been a long five to seven years. Success factors for this part of Leviton's business include economies of scale and close relationships with the major downstream distributors. Economies of scale are achieved through Leviton's dominant share position, the close distribution relationships are solidified by Leviton's leadership role in EDI (Electronic Data Interchange), the systems that glue suppliers, distributors, and customers together in almost a seamless fashion.

With the dawning of the home improvement boom in the U.S., a fashionable wiring device industry also emerged. Baby boomers, redoing their patios, wanted rustic light switches and receptacles that were weather resistant, and in the dining room, dimmer switches to adjust the evening mood to the occasion. This fashion device part of Leviton's business has a shorter product life cycle of three to five years. Differences in product life cycle, marketing, and distribution requirements led Leviton to house this product line in a separate fashion conscious division, a division organized to churn out new models more frequently to harvest the changing moods of homeowners and businesses around the nation.

The next major change to the wiring device industry came with new electronic switch technologies. These enabled the development of low-cost switches activated by light, sound, and electronic coupling, for which human hands are not required. Product development in this business involves a whole new array of skills (sensor technology, new materials capabilities) and more advanced manufacturing competencies. Even so, Leviton managers can leverage their massive distribution and customer base to boot-strap themselves into this expanding high-tech business. The product life cycle for this business is also much shorter: one to three years.

As Leviton entered this third business, it became obvious that the wire frame CADAM design system running on the Amdahl 5990 model 700 and connected to IBM terminals was not keeping up. Designers had a difficult time visualizing end-products when they were drafted in two dimensions. Prototypes were painstakingly created only to be reworked as designers noticed important differences between their vision of the end-product and the part under development. Engineers became increasingly frustrated as they came under the gun to meet the now much tighter deadlines imposed by the newer businesses.

Mr. Oddsen saw part of the solution in adopting three-dimensional solid modeling systems for producing realistic prototype images on high resolution screens early in the development process. The newer 3-D visuals would provide a tangible enough image for designers and developers to sign off on before prototyping. Excessive prototyping could thereby be avoided and better products could be developed. Major design changes could be made at the initial stages, when flexibility is greatest. Quality throughout the process would improve and, in turn, lead to increased productivity and lower costs. Mr. Oddsen calculated that average development time could drop by half.

Upgrading the mainframe to obtain processing power for 3-D modeling was explored, but quickly dismissed as it became clear that engineering workstations now packed enough power to get the job done at a fraction of the cost. HP and several other vendor offerings were assessed before deciding on 80 HP workstations with an HP server running HP's ME CAD software. The deciding factor, according to Mr. Oddsen, was ease of use. His developers felt the interface of the HP software was intuitive enough to allow even newer engineers to be productive soon after sitting down at the keyboard.

At first, the plan was to move to HP over a three-year period, but the economics of the move were attractive enough and the ease of transition was such that plans were shortened to six to nine months. This move will take all engineering design operations completely off the mainframe. Once liberated from the mainframe, Mr. Oddsen is planning to look into prototyping equipment (perhaps using lasers) for translating the 3-D images into physical models for an additional level of design certainty at the beginning of the design process.

It was not long before questions were being asked at Leviton concerning the feasibility of taking the engineering downsizing experience and applying it to commercial systems as well. Expansion of Leviton's business has placed additional strain on the mainframe and an estimate for upgrade costs to meet the expanded commercial processing demands exceeds $.5 million for hardware and software combined. Stephen Hiller, Leviton's VP of Information Systems, is investigating alternatives for commercial system downsizing and is not without concerns as he sifts through his options. He does not think unplugging his commercial mainframe is a realistic alternative. He expects it will always be necessary as a communication and database server, especially in the area of EDI and order entry. Leviton has pushed mainframe application technology close to the limit for providing decision support information across the company by carefully integrating applications on the host. Mr. Hiller comments, "Managers with the appropriate security clearance can get most of the information they need on development, manufacturing, inventories, orders, etc., because we have emphasized cross-functional integration of applications and data in our mainframe software development efforts."

Mr. Hiller is mostly concerned about open systems transaction processing capabilities, a major requirement of Leviton's business environment. Another important issue for Leviton is avoiding having to discard the mainframe code that has served them so well over the years. Luckily, much of Mr. Hiller's code runs in Software AG's Adabase environment, one of the tools that has been fully migrated to the open systems environment. A final concern is how to change the mindset of MIS staff members who have excelled in resolving difficult business and system problems with mainframe technology. It is only natural that mainframe solutions continue to come first to their minds, even on the newer development programs.

Mr. Hiller, however, is not going to let these concerns get in the way of moving ahead. He has already identified E-mail, general ledger, forecasting, distribution resource planning, and customer support systems as potential candidates for newer distributed computing platforms. As he moves, he expects 4GL tools to ease the transition for his staff by taking care of the memory management and multi-tasking challenges characteristic of the downsized environment. He exhibits a cautious, but positive attitude as he thinks about the challenges ahead. His plans are to "pick a small application and do it! not analyze it to death." After that experience he will have a better understanding of what his real concerns should be in moving from concurrent engineering to concurrent commercial computing.

How About Going for Zero Inventory?

Wal-Mart and Acustar

How could any retailer achieve zero inventory, you say? Well, published accomplishments by Wal-Mart, the aggressive discount retail chain, come about as close as you can get. At Wal-Mart, the stores are equipped with satellite dish communication for voice, data, and video communication with 17 Wal-Mart regional distribution centers. Customer purchases are recorded by bar code, in-store computers monitor the daily sales, shelf turnover, and inventory levels for transmission via the satellite link. This information is automatically translated into purchase orders submitted directly through EDI links to Wal-Mart's suppliers, and the suppliers replenish the shelves with just-in-time efficiency. In fact, the orders submitted electronically to Procter & Gamble, one of Wal-Mart's largest suppliers, at the end of the day, are often delivered that same night, to be available for the hordes of discount shoppers beating their way to Wal-Mart's doors every morning. Wal-Mart used HP midrange and workstation open systems to build most of this strategic information system showcase.

Another company, this one in the automobile components industry, was able to dramatically lower manufacturing inventory using downsized open systems in a different way—by moving inventory control and decision-making down to the plant manager level.

Imagine being a plant manager for Acustar, a supplier of seat covers, wire harnesses, and other components to Chrysler, GM, and Isuzu in late 1991. You run one of eight plants operated by Acustar just across the border from the U.S. in Mexico. The inventory management program operates on a mainframe in Hunstville, Alabama, and no one in your factory can access the mainframe directly. Your only access is by calling managers at the regional headquarters in El Paso, and asking them to read you information over the phone. Information on parts deliveries and work-in-process/finished goods inventories at your site is transmitted to El Paso by phone, fax, or mail, where it is input by hand. Needless to say, when Acustar headquarters started applying pressure to reduce parts and work-in-process inventories at the Mexican plants, there was little that could be said besides, "We'll try our best." Without appropriate information on goods and materials flow, the only job that could really be done was day-to-day managing of the local Mexican workers.

In those days, Acustar's formula for cost reduction was out of balance. Labor costs were kept low through the use of inexpensive Mexican labor, but labor in the automobile components industry made up less than 20% of the overall costs. The much larger raw materials and inventory cost component (over 70% of the total), was climbing out of control. The laws of "just-in-case" usually take over in situations like these and Acustar was no exception. Plant managers ordered extra materials to ensure that parts would be available to keep the lines running. Ballooning buffer inventories resulted, crowding warehouses and factories, but without effective and timely tracking mechanisms, there was little that could be done.

Acustar's information systems tangle had gradually worsened over a 12-year span as the number of Mexican plants expanded from one to eight. It was not until 1991, however, when Chrysler purchased a nearby wire assembly plant from American Motors and slated it for consolidation with the El Paso office, that the situation became so untenable that a complete information system revamp was seriously considered.

You can probably guess the happy ending to this story. Just like many of the other companies discussed in this book, Acustar brought in distributed open systems (from HP), applied appropriate software packages (CMI's Competitive Solutions Inventory Control and MRP packages), and hooked up the factories directly to the inventory and material data housed on a server in El Paso. The El Paso server, in turn, was connected via an SNA link to the Alabama mainframe. An EDI linkage was also put in place to communicate directly with Chrysler.

With the new system, the plant managers were able to meet low inventory levels previously considered unattainable in just a few short months. To be exact, they achieved their two-year goal in seven months time and then went on to achieve additional stretch goals just to see just how far they could go. Plant managers could finally use their management skills to knock off inventory problems one by one, starting on areas promising the highest positive impact. They could now manage the flow of goods in and out, and eliminate "just-in-case" inventory float from a high of 20 days in many areas to, in some cases, less than 5 days. The plant managers finally had the confidence to manage the flow of inventory to plants located 700 miles way at the slimmest margins because they had everything under control using real-time data on what had been shipped, received, and produced. They did this all without even picking up the phone. When they did pick up the phone in El Paso to talk with the factories, the conversations were much more effective. The same computer charts could be pulled up at both locations and communication could transcend the language barriers they had been putting up with for years. Superfluous questions from the plant concerning how to use the information system fell to a minimum and were replaced by more important business and operational inquiries, such as, "How do you think we can eliminate the excess material being delivered by that supplier?"

Acustar plant managers see themselves at the start of a whole new era of information systems working for them, rather than against them. El Paso management has created an MIS function to focus solely on "plant system development programs." They are incorporating new applications for such activities as linking material receipts with accounts payable, processing payroll at the plants, and achieving more effectiveness from the low-cost labor pool through direct labor performance applications.

This has not gone unnoticed by Chrysler. Chrysler has already ordered another HP UNIX system to be installed in a Detroit operation producing plastic parts for a new line of Chrysler automobiles and trucks. Apparently, their ballooning buffer inventories need puncturing as well.

Replicate! Replicate! Replicate!

ITT Sheraton

When geographically dispersed systems are made up of dumb terminals and data links, few systems engineers ever need to wander out of the glass house. Distributed computing as we have seen from previous examples, pulls many of the engineers out into very unfamiliar territory, i.e., the user community. Anxiety concerning the complexity of the new dispersed system, and the unfamiliarity of the new environment, is often a formidable barrier to overcome in making the change. Nevertheless, new methodologies are lowering this barrier by making certain tasks, such as installing geographically dispersed subsystems for a hotel chain, less daunting than one might expect. ITT Sheraton's six-month roll-out of over 300 integrated reservation systems in their U.S. hotels would be unthinkable without replicated site technology. Once the networking is in place, the system modules fit together like pieces of a jigsaw puzzle, and the roll-out becomes automatic.

ITT Sheraton's new system effort was prompted by serious shortcomings in the communication link between their central and local hotel reservation systems. ITT Sheraton reservation agents could not always be as certain as they would like about local hotel room availability. Most of the hotels were franchise-owned, and although most of the locations in the U.S. had similar NCR tower systems, the systems themselves were not designed to provide on-line, or even on-time information.

The newly recruited Senior VP and Chief Information Systems Officer, Richard L. Nauman, and his team took a hard look at the mainframe and found that only an upgrade would deliver the added functionality and capacity ITT Sheraton needed. They soon realized that Amdahl mainframes could do the job for less, and so ITT Sheraton quickly made the switch to Amdahl, and then explored options for filling out the rest of the system.

Rather than just building a reservation system, the MIS team had their sights on eventually creating a fully integrated reservation, property management, and customer marketing operation that would give ITT Sheraton a competitive edge far out into the 90s. To accomplish this, they needed to build an infrastructure for the future—one not only acceptable to ITT Sheraton Corporate, but also to all the independent-minded franchise owners as well.

The team felt the time was right to tie all the customer information available throughout the hotel chain into an integrated pool of knowledge for better serving Sheraton customers. Knowing what type of customers stay most often, use the most services, and spend the most money is important for putting together preferred customer programs aimed at locking in frequent stayers. Information on the typical preferred customer profile (title, company size, whether reservations are made via travel department or directly, etc.) would direct Sheraton marketing efforts toward the right customers and influencers. Knowing what services frequent customers use and prefer would also allow Sheraton to create competitive programs with true appeal to preferred guests, rather than be stuck producing me-too services, based on those originated by competitors. Finally, monitoring this type of information allows for tracking the effectiveness of ongoing promotion efforts, and making timely mid-course corrections.

It was clear to ITT Sheraton MIS managers from the start that the distributed "brains" of the system had to be first class. They found that the INFORMIX relational database had all the necessary functions at an appropriate price. Then they searched for hardware platforms which would effectively support INFORMIX. Price performance, scalability, and global support structure were also important considerations. Mr. Nauman says that HP-UX systems won on all these counts. Finally came the selection of an appropriate property management software package. His team chose a package from ECI that did not run on HP. Not to worry, Sheraton worked with ECI to port and enhance the software for running on the HP platform, based on anticipated software volumes from the program.

A major hurdle still remained, however. The franchise hotel owners had to be brought on-board through a series of intense sessions. Luckily, the franchise owners were sufficiently fed up with the prior system to vote in the new platform. The system roll-out was for the most part without incident. Individual server sizes were matched to the volume of business at each hotel. No matter what size server, the software was exactly the same. The largest ITT Sheraton Hotels (referred to as "Super Tankers") were found to be candidates for HP's highest-end mainframe replacement servers. Mr. Nauman expects the newly announced HP Emerald Corporate Business Server system (equivalent in power to an IBM 3090 600J) to be able to run the entire operation.

Now that the first set of systems are in place, the ITT Sheraton MIS managers have two more implementation phases ahead of them. Phase 2 will herald the start of the newly integrated property management system to be housed on the same server platforms (Sheraton is developing the code), and with Phase 3, the infrastructure for the next generation guest marketing programs will be completed. After that it will be replicate! replicate! replicate! as all current and future domestic and international Sheraton franchise hotels are brought into the distributed information system fold.

Creating New Markets through Information Technology

Paychex

Information technology has not only helped expand existing businesses but has also spawned totally new industries and markets. Operations that at first appeared to be too costly to be profitable, become feasible when computer systems are employed. The newer distributed computing technologies which allow for even greater efficiency and flexibility are beginning to open up new avenues for existing businesses, and it is likely that these same technologies will give birth to new billion dollar markets over the next few years.

Paychex, a payroll processing firm based in Rochester, New York, used borrowed mainframe MIPs and distributed computing technology to build a highly profitable business out of paycheck issuing and reporting for companies with fewer than 100 employees. These companies were previously ignored as too small to be served profitably by the traditional payroll processing industry. Paychex is now shifting to open systems and client/server technologies to continue its expansion and create new engines for company growth. The Paychex story is one of entrepreneurial spirit backed by successive waves of lower cost information technology.

Imagine I am a Paychex Sales Representative and you are a small restaurant owner in the U.S. with 17 employees. Now imagine all the bookkeeping and report filing required by the federal government, state and local government, insurance companies, etc. Paychex estimates that the typical small business employer in New York state is burdened with as many as 42 federal and state payroll tax filings each year, in addition to the regular tasks of payroll deduction calculations and paycheck issuing each pay period. In other states, such as Pennsylvania and Ohio, the number of reports can exceed 50. Late or misfiled reports lead to expensive penalties and late charge interest fees excised on hapless businesses with less than orderly records.

Imagine the amount of time spent by yourself as the small business owner or your staff to keep records straight and up-to-date. Let's say you spend six hours preparing each of the 42 reports, plus eight hours preparing for each of the 52 pay periods. That is 668 hours (16.7 five-day work weeks) total. If you or your staff are doing this with calculators, pens and pencils today, you are probably applying $31,000 to this task (16.7 weeks/48 annual work weeks for an employee whose salary and benefits equal $90,000). More cost could also be added to this total to account for the aggravation and penalties extracted by the government for inadvertent reporting errors.

Now imagine I visit you as the Paychex Sales Representative and tell you that Paychex can take care of all your payroll difficulties, including record-keeping, check issuing, tax filing, and report generation for only $23 per pay period (less than $1.50 per employee), and that Paychex is a reliable company already serving over 100,000 customers with timely and accurate service. The yearly cost to you would be around $1,200 (versus the $31,000 calculated above, or if you are twice as efficient as the above formula, $15,500). Would you be interested?

This is the underlying value proposition that has driven Paychex from being a start-up with $3,000 capital 20 years ago to becoming a "Wall Street Darling" growth company averaging 20% growth per year, achieving $161 million in 1992 revenue (with a healthy 8.5% net income percent), and returning an enviable 22.5%

to stockholders' equity. Paychex's market appears to be almost unlimited. 98% of U.S. companies have fewer than 100 employees (Paychex's target market). The power of Paychex's value proposition is evidenced by the extraordinary productivity achieved by their sales reps. Many can sign up 200 new customers per year (close to four a week). The best have signed up 400 to 500 new customers two years in a row in the Rochester area alone. This productivity is achieved mostly through referrals from CPAs and satisfied customers.

Paychex is receiving nationwide recognition these days. Prestigious *Forbes* magazine lists Paychex as number 80 on its ranking of the 200 best-managed companies with revenues of less than $350 million. Paychex also gained a place on *Business Week's* ranking of the top 1,000 most valuable U.S. companies in terms of share market value (outstanding shares times price per share). Not bad for a company picking up customers other payroll processing companies by-passed as too small to be profitable. How did Paychex do it?

The entrepreneur, Tom Golisano, who placed the $3,000 down to start the Paychex dream, has been written up extensively in local and national publications. He is, without a doubt, a true street-fighting entrepreneur with a close eye on his customers, an excellent knack for picking stellar business opportunities (Paychex is just one of his many ventures), and a strong sense of what is necessary to ensure his value proposition stays intact over time. His payroll specialists are reminded of Mr. Golisano's value proposition through weekly training sessions, tests taken at the end of each session, and by taking Paychex exams every quarter to ensure they are up-to-date on payroll and related tax regulations, as well as expected customer questions.

Mr. Golisano skillfully evaded many of the start-up pitfalls that sink most small companies as they grow. Early on, he leveraged the entrepreneurial spirit of his most trusted friends by setting them up with franchise and partnership operations (new territories all to themselves) around the country. The first was Syracuse, then Miami and Florida, and one year later, Detroit, Cleveland, and Los Angeles. By 1979, he had established 19 franchise or joint venture partners in 26 cities. He soon discovered important weaknesses in this approach when the business started taking on a truly nationwide scope (difficult to control quality of offering across partnerships, partners could not "cash in" easily when they decided to retire or move on, the necessary nationwide information systems infrastructure was difficult to fund) and acted quickly to consolidate the group of start-ups into one umbrella corporation. He first conducted a group meeting in the Bahamas. Later in a series of one-on-one meetings with each of the partners, Mr. Golisano convinced this group of fiercely independent and successful managers to turn in their titles of company "President" for "Vice President" under himself. After celebrating the union, he then set some tough revenue and profit hurdles for all. These were achieved and he was able to take the company public, even during a relatively soft stock market in 1983.

Since that time, Mr. Golisano has expanded the number of customers to 160,000 businesses and increased the number of services beyond payroll to include direct deposit, human resource programs, and tax payments and filing. The system infrastructure put in place for payroll opened the way for the expansion to other services, and the newer services leverage the infrastructure to provide even higher profitability. Tax filing, for instance, generates an additional float that may be insignificant to the small business owner, but is handsomely profitable when consolidated from 50,000 small business accounts.

What does all of this have to do with information technology? The Paychex story smacks of "rags to riches" inspiration for would-be entrepreneurs searching for a formula for success—a formula that could be a charismatic leadership quality or perhaps a philosophy that permeates the personality and actions of the truly successful business builder. The Paychex story can also be seen as an example of the true power of underlying information technology when placed in the hands of an individual with all of the personal qualities for success. Let me try to document the heretofore unwritten information technology story behind the rapid and profitable growth of Paychex.

First, one basic question: Would Paychex exist today if there were only mainframe technology at the company's disposal for processing payroll? Not according to Bob Beegen, Paychex's head of MIS and partner from the early Paychex years. He tells a story of how Paychex had to borrow unused MIPs on Honeywell and IBM mainframes to process payrolls during the initial cash-starved years for the company, and then how Paychex quickly drove down transaction costs further by riding the waves of distributed computing with minicomputers. Now, Mr. Beegen is leading the charge to open systems and client/server technology in order to add functionality for the new businesses, while maintaining costs per transaction well under the average Paychex charge to the customer of $1.83.

Tom Golisano first got the idea for Paychex when he was working in the early 1970s for EAS, a Rochester-based accounting and payroll processing company, serving larger company needs. Typical practice in those days was to charge base fees (minimum period charges) that made it uneconomical for smaller companies to join up. When his suggestions to start up a small-company payroll processing business within EAS were rebuffed, he decided to go out on his own and became a volume customer on EAS's tape-based Honeywell 1200 series systems, processing payrolls for his start-up business. Payrolls for the Cleveland and Los Angeles businesses were processed at EAS in Rochester, and the Syracuse branch manager processed his payrolls at a local Syracuse EAS office. Bob Beegen obtained a Honeywell payroll system application and modified it so the output would resemble the EAS format. He then bought time at a local clinic in Detroit to process the customer payrolls at his Detroit Paychex operation.

Tom Golisano and Bob Beegen soon realized that Paychex needed to move away from using Honeywell systems. Limited market presence would undermine Honeywell's ongoing ability to provide low-cost systems incorporating the newest technologies. They were aware of lower cost platforms from other vendors that could meet the demands of the growing business and still maintain low enough costs per transaction for Paychex's target market.

Tom Golisano went to great lengths to fund Paychex system development. Articles on the "Paychex story" tell how he overran his personal credit card limits with company charges during the first two to three lean years of operation. They also describe how he borrowed money from his sister, Marie, in mid-1975 to fund "important software development and buy the hardware for it to run on." Ms. Golisano withdrew the money from her life insurance proceeds and did not get it back until Paychex started breaking even in 1979. Mr. Golisano and Mr. Beegen selected the IBM System 3 as their platform and developed a custom payroll processing system to run on it.

Mr. Beegen started this next phase of Paychex payroll processing by buying time at $25 per hour on a System 3 at the local Real Estate board, and later was able to purchase an in-house system for batch runs in Detroit. He could not, however, find a suitably low-cost platform to meet Paychex's longer term objectives of sustainable growth and profitability until less expensive minicomputers became available in the late 70s.

In 1983, Mr. Beegen converted Paychex to a distributed computing topology based on Prime minicomputers at "half the cost of an alternative IBM 4300 series system." These systems were not only lower cost, but due to their interactive capability, they were a more effective platform for reducing Paychex's most important costs—data input proofing/editing.

Prior to the Prime system, Paychex payroll specialists were required to record entries on paper timesheets using complex instructions. The sheets were then entered on cards or disks for processing on IBM equipment with no local editing. Input errors were difficult to detect and adjust. The batch runs would sometimes take hours to correct and rerun. Many weekends were consumed by endless hours of monotonous computer tasks. Not surprisingly, the turnover for payroll specialists exceeded 50% in the early years. The stress was just too much.

With the Prime system, Paychex was able to rescue the specialists. A Prime 2250 series mini with six to eight terminals, 320 megabytes of disk storage, and two megabytes of main memory was placed at each branch office. The average system configuration cost was $70,000, and object level compatibility among Prime's systems allowed for smooth upgrades as processing requirements increased in subsequent years.

The new input and editing screens were well-liked by the specialists. Paychex monitors still use the four different screens developed on the Prime systems for over-the-telephone data input and editing. In addition to minimizing editing time (the major cost drain), the newer interface made specialist training much easier and improved employee retention considerably. Operator turnover declined from the earlier 50% average to a much more manageable 25%. After installing the new systems in 1983, Paychex's net profit percent grew from a mediocre 5.6% to a stellar 8.2% in 1986, and then to 9.3% in 1989. Paychex's net profit percent in 1992 was 8.5%. Not all of this, of course, can be ascribed to the type of information system installed. The five-fold increase in revenues over this period from $23 million to $101 million (and to $161 million in 1992) also played an important role by providing better bottom line economies of scale. Nevertheless, 40% of Paychex's costs are information systems-related. As Bob Beegen puts it, a bad information systems decision could easily "sink the ship." One such potentially bad decision, according to Bob Beegen, would have been to stay with IBM. He comments, "The IBM alternative was twice the price. There is no way we could have grown the business as we have with that kind of informa-tion systems cost."

With so much weight on his shoulders you might expect Mr. Beegen to be ultra-conservative in his system decisions. Mr. Beegen feels, however, that newer system technologies are essential drivers of the functionality and cost models for succeeding in Paychex's businesses. His job, in his mind, is to stay on top of newer technolo-gies to ensure sufficient control of technology risks, as Paychex breaks newer computing ground. Mr. Beegen has just installed 70 new HP9000 UNIX servers with terminals in Paychex branches equipped with Oracle relational database software and tools. He is also currently exploring an object-oriented environment and data-base using Oracle. He claims that the new systems cost exactly the same as the Prime systems he installed ten years earlier ($70,000 per set), but "have many magnitudes higher performance and much more functionality."

Mr. Beegen's joint work with Oracle also places him on the lead-ing edge with respect to object-oriented technology. He sees the indi-vidual check as the most appropriate "object" for processing in Paychex's business. He comments, "There are an infinite number of variations with respect to what can happen to a check transaction. If checks become identifiable objects in the system, and check objects can be modified without knowing where the related records or appli-cations are, the entire system can be much more effective and easier to use." Oracle managers have promised Mr. Beegen that they will provide a bridge from their current database to the future object-ori-ented version.

Why the change away from Prime? In 1988, when Mr. Beegen returned from leading a multi-year new product development pro-gram to, in his words, "render order out of chaos," it became clear to him that Paychex needed to undergo substantial change. Paychex had run out of head room with Prime's object-compatible systems. Moving to the next larger Prime system would require recompiling most of Paychex's software. Mr. Beegen saw the writing on the wall when he tried to run his new benefits services program on Oracle using the largest Prime platform and found the Prime machine com-pletely consumed by the application. The same application ran faster on a small IBM PS2 model 60! He diagnosed the problem as "serious server blockage" occurring on the Prime.

Other problems had also surfaced with the Prime systems. From Mr. Beegen's perspective, Prime "had gone out of their way to be as nonstandard as possible." They had, for instance, "placed sign indicator bits in a different sequence from all other vendors." The Prime systems served Paychex's needs in the early 80s, but lack of connectivity and interoperability among Prime platforms had begun to seriously hinder productivity. Tax filing, human resources management, telemarketing, etc., had all come on-line and it did not make sense to place the software on every system in each of the branch offices to overcome the lack of Prime interoperability. Prime's systems also could not take full advantage of Oracle's ability to support both on-line transaction processing and batch on the same CPU, and both types of applications were necessary at each Paychex office location.

Other Prime customers had also apparently begun to switch to other vendors because of Prime's weaknesses causing Prime's market share to erode. Paychex did not want to stay locked in to a vendor who could not command sufficient market pull to attract ISVs with the newest software tools and applications to their platform. Mr. Beegen saw it was time to check out the next wave of distributed computing technology. As he explored his options, he became dead set on also moving to open systems. He believes open systems eliminate the need to "have a crystal ball" when choosing a hardware platform. "Who knows what hardware will be best 10 years from today?" Mr. Beegen wondered out loud in a recent interview.

Mr. Beegen studied the leading-edge UNIX vendors and chose HP9000 servers. HP's rapidly expanding market share, commitment to open systems, and superior price performance clinched the decision. Sequent fell off the list due to the significantly higher cost of its platform.

The HP systems have just been installed, and Mr. Beegen anticipates having an open field for meeting future Paychex needs, regardless of what they turn out to be. Already he is taking advantage of Net Blazers to achieve extra payroll processing reliability by automatically rerouting communications if lines go down. His newer networks also provide for substantial communications cost reduction through data compression at 16300 baud on inexpensive seven cent-per-connection-minute lines. The Oracle platform on HP servers provides him much more than just the handling of on-line transaction processing and batch on the same CPU. Oracles's overall flexibility and functionality are allowing him to enhance current specialist screens to provide such features as context-sensitive help and other updated operation instructions. These capabilities will be fully deployed on painted screens across the system when Paychex's object-oriented database is completed over the next couple of years.

Mr. Beegen acknowledges that not all the necessary system management tools and utilities exist yet for the new open systems environment, but he is convinced that when they arrive they will be on HP. He is also convinced that Paychex should not wait for the tools. He observes, "Unless we experiment with the tools that exist today and adjust them as necessary to meet our needs, we won't have sufficient in-house expertise to assess future tools when they are introduced. Companies that do not start now, and wait for future fixes to current open systems shortcomings, will be once more behind the power curve in terms of system expertise and be at the mercy of their hardware and software vendors, even in the new open systems environment! I feel that open systems is more than plug and play software components—open systems provide the opportunity to customize systems to a company's needs, without locking the company into a specific vendor platform."

Mr. Beegen has definite plans for the future, but is keeping them as quiet as his boss, Tom Golisano. When Mr. Golisano was asked by a reporter from the *Rochester Business Magazine* whether he had any ideas for new business ventures, he simply replied "Yes" and chuckled. When this author suggested to Mr. Beegen that his network could perhaps link small businesses all over the country and serve as a platform for all types of communication, information, and administration services, and that he perhaps did not need to stop there, and could venture into the home market, he responded with a knowing gleam in his eye.

Conclusion

The early-adopting IT-preneurs are certainly out in force. The MIS directors interviewed for this book, for the most part, fall into this category. They aren't waiting for vendors to finish paving the highway to their IT future. They're rolling up their sleeves to work with vendors to ensure the IT highway has the infrastructure necessary for bolstering their businesses, e.g., a solid road bed (commercial robustness), appropriate road width and the right number of lanes (broadband networking), convenient exits (interoperability), easily understood road signs (ease of use), etc. These IT-preneurs are taking charge, and HP is continually benefitting from the hints and suggestions they generously provide.

Bob Beegan of Paychex, for instance, told this author that he has some ideas for minimizing source code overhead in HP's OpenSpool and OpenView system software. His team has apparently made some helpful fixes he would like to share. Roger Dyer of GE Information Systems has a team of developers who have created a multiprocessing operating system that exhibits remarkable performance across multiple mainframes. Mr. Dyer's team is now working with HP to ensure HP systems can meet GEIS's stringent requirements for application software firewalls in similar configurations of multiple UNIX servers.

It is natural that the more proactive MIS managers are the first to take advantage of new technology waves. Many of them have also been the first to adopt earlier innovations, e.g., the minicomputer, the PC, parallel processing, etc. However, past IT waves have often left companies questioning the true business benefits of their IT investments. Not so this time. IT-preneurs downsizing to open systems are benefiting from the double whammy of information system cost reduction and the dramatic expansion of business value. Lite-line representatives providing replenishment advice to downstream retailers will now be able to provide that service with much greater accuracy at lower IS cost. ITT Sheraton reservation agents will provide highly personalized service without requiring increased use of expensive mainframe MIPs.

With this next wave of technology, information systems will finally emerge as a business force that can either underpin or undermine the success of any company. What does this mean for MIS directors who subscribe to the theory that it is best to wait for technologies to become mainstream before trying them out? And what about the MIS managers who are so afraid of the bleeding edge that they never even look at cutting edge technology?

We are already seeing the consequences for some of the slower movers. Articles abound about revolving CIO doors. Many of the stories in this book feature the accomplishments of new MIS directors installed to make a difference in their company's IT future. Dick Wright was placed in charge at Simmonds Precision to spearhead an MIS cultural change, the newly hired "Ian Inman" brought unprecedented dynamism to the role of MIS at "Delight" (the sign which still graces the "Delight" MIS office door is a holdover from the old MIS role; it labels the department "Programmers"), and "Mike Mickel" was brought in after "Mediply" was acquired to revamp its IS infrastructure.

Moving slowly is not the more conservative path anymore, it is now the riskier strategy. Downsizing technology is bringing IT magic to life as it plays the role of a benevolent genie, granting the information access wishes of employees throughout IT-enlightened companies. The wishes of these employees, however, are just as often directed at taking away the customers of less IT-enlightened competitors. Postponing the move to downsized systems means a company will be that much later in employing its own genie, that much more likely to lose out in the next business shake out, and that much more a candidate for being transformed from "strong business predator" into "hapless prey" as it misses the technology boat.

The upside to this equation is the emergence of bountiful information technology opportunities for heretofore underdog companies to leverage in turning the tables on more powerful competitors. If strategic initiatives by your company have been repeatedly quashed by Goliath competitors with vast economies of scale at their disposal, perhaps you can use IT to redefine the battlefield. Can IT-based services, for instance, provide your downstream customers greater savings or revenues than they can derive from purchasing slightly lower priced competitor products? Can your quality be more dependable and deliveries better timed to customer needs than competitors who are using out-of-date information systems? Will customers feel more comfortable dealing with a firm that has made all relevant account information easily accessible to customer representatives answering incoming calls? Is there a better time than now, when discontinuous change is reaching an all time high in the IT world, to make your move?

I feel extremely fortunate be a witness at this critical juncture of business and information technology worlds. It is a point in time when a company's ability to leverage newer IT technologies can determine its future business success. The existence or lack of this capability could be a useful parameter for Wall Street firms to assess long-term buy, hold and sell recommendations. When Tom Peters and Bob Waterman selected "excellent" companies to feature in their book, *In Search of Excellence,* they included HP. One strength these authors identified as special to HP was excellent communication between management members and employees, exemplified by MBWA (Management By Walking Around). MBWA was coined by John Doyle, HP's recently retired Senior Vice President, to describe HP's wide open door policy. The wide open door of HP, however, can now be made even wider through the newer IT technologies. Networks, for instance, can be created by IT-preneurs to allow management teams to electronically "walk around" every part of their vast company, customer, and supplier worlds. Interaction with top executives will no longer need to be relegated to corporate memos, large hall speeches, and small meetings with select groups. Their guidance, encouragement, and insights can be tapped dynamically by the whole company. This form of ubiquity is not only provided to top management, but also to all employees of the company so that experts can share expertise across the enterprise, and groups can work together without organizational, or geographic barriers.

My reading of the situation is that there is little time to waste. What is yours?

Index